A Future for Small States

Overcoming Vulnerability

Report by a Commonwealth Advisory Group

Dame Eugenia Charles

Mr Andreas Jacovides

Hon Ms Fiamé Naomi Mata'afa

Mr Ken Ross

Mr Tim Thahane

Mr Natarajan Krishnan

Dr Edgar Mizzi

H E Professor Havelock Ross-Brewster

Mr Taniela Tufui

COMMONWEALTH SECRETARIAT

All enquiries for assistance should be directed to:
The Director
Economic Affairs Division
Commonwealth Secretariat
Marlborough House
Pall Mall
London SW1Y 5HX
Britain

Tel: +44 (0)171-747 6261/6231
Fax: +44 (0)171-747 6235

Commonwealth Secretariat
Marlborough House
Pall Mall
London SW1Y 5HX
Britain

Published by the Commonwealth Secretariat
Designed by TSGD
Indexed by Sue Martin
Printed in Britain by Formara Limited
Wherever possible, the Commonwealth Secretariat uses paper that is made
from sustainable forests or from sources that minimise is a destructive impact
on the environment.

ISBN: 0-85092-511-8   Price: £12.99

Contents

List of Tables

Foreword by the Commonwealth Secretary-General

Over the years, the Commonwealth has played an important role as advocate for small states' issues and contributed to greater international awareness of the particular vulnerabilities and special needs of these countries. In this regard, a seminal contribution was the 1985 Commonwealth report, *Vulnerability: Small States in the Global Society.* This report raised the political profile of small states' issues in international fora. The international context faced by these countries has changed dramatically since the Cold War ended. At the second meeting of the Ministerial Group on Small States held in Auckland in 1995, Ministers recognised this and concluded that recent international developments pointed to the need for small states' vulnerability to be analysed in all its dimensions to cover political, economic, social and environmental concerns.

Ministers therefore called for an updating of the *Vulnerability* report to address the fundamental global changes since 1985, in areas such as international trade, sustainable development and new threats to small states' security.

In order to prepare the new report, and after consultations with member governments, I constituted an Advisory Group of eminent persons to reflect the diversity of the Commonwealth. I was fortunate in being able to bring together a group with a wealth of knowledge from around the Commonwealth. The Group was supported by two excellent resource persons, Dr Paul Sutton and Professor David Pearce, as well as the Secretariat. Under the able guidance of its chairperson, Dame Eugenia Charles, former Prime Minister of Dominica, the nine-member Group completed a challenging task in a remarkably short period of time.

The Advisory Group met twice in London in May and July 1997. At its first meeting, the Group agreed to pursue the investigation and analysis of a range of concerns facing small states. These included the possible marginalisation of small economies as a result of the progressive liberalisation of the global economy and the growing trend towards regionalism; likely disastrous consequences for small states resulting from global warming and climate change, and environmental fragility; vulnerability to criminal activities, such as money laundering and drug trafficking; and possible threats to security arising from the transboundary movement of hazardous waste and nuclear material.

At its second meeting, the Group discussed further and completed its report, incorporating a series of practical and achievable recommendations on globalisation, environment and political security for action at national, regional, international and Commonwealth levels. Their assessment and recommendations provide important guiding principles for mainstreaming small states' issues in international fora, as well as for designing programmes for action at all levels.

I am pleased to commend the Report, A *Future for Small States: Overcoming Vulnerability*, and its recommendations to Commonwealth Governments and to the wider international community.

Emeka Anyaoku

Emeka Anyaoku
30 July 1997

Letter of Presentation

Marlborough House
London

16 July 1997

Chief Emeka Anyaoku
Commonwealth Secretary-General
Marlborough House
London SW1Y 5HX

Dear Secretary-General

In accordance with the decision of the Commonwealth Consultative Group of Senior Officials on Small States (CGSS), you appointed us as a group of independent experts to revise and update the 1985 Commonwealth Report, *Vulnerability: Small States in the Global Society*. In completing this assignment, we have focused not only on the vulnerability of these states but also on other relevant factors affecting their security and development.

We transmit herewith our Report which represents the unanimous conclusions and recommendations of the Group. The report is a collective effort containing a wealth of descriptive and analytical material which has been meticulously assembled by the consultants under the guidance of the Secretariat to whom we are deeply indebted. In accordance with the terms of our appointment, we have signed the Report in our personal capacities and not as representatives of governments, organisations or countries to which we belong.

We are in no doubt that this period of political, economic, social and environmental change presents both complex challenges and great opportunities for small nations in the international community. Going a little further, we would venture that small states need not necessarily be seen as a burden on the international community but rather as a source of enrichment. It is our earnest hope that our conclusions will help to re-kindle interest and focus attention on the particular vulnerabilities of small states and their prospects, and that they will inspire the global community to give the concerns of these countries the attention they deserve in major international fora. It is our belief that the Commonwealth is well-placed to take a leading role in bringing this about.

We are grateful to you for the confidence which you have shown in appointing us to carry out this important task. We are also grateful to your staff, including the consultants, for their unfailing assistance and we would like, through you, to express our gratitude to all concerned.

Yours sincerely,

Dame Eugenia Charles

Hon (Ms) Fiame Naomi Mata'afa

Mr Tim Thahane

H E Mr Havelock Ross-Brewster

Ambassador Andreas Jacovides

Mr N Krishnan

Mr Taniela Tufui

Mr Ken Ross

Dr Edgar Mizzi

Executive Summary and Recommendations

1. This report identifies the characteristics which most shape the security concerns of small states, particularly those that render them vulnerable: openness, insularity or 'enclaveness', resilience, weakness and dependence. Consideration is given to the economic, environmental and geopolitical dimensions of small state security. The report examines measures small states can take to improve their national capacity and international presence. Small states have a population of 1.5 million or less. There are 32 small states in the Commonwealth.

2. Small states have a susceptibility to risks and threats set at a relatively lower threshold than for larger states. The major threats faced by small states are to their territorial integrity and security; political independence and security; economic security; environmental sustainability; and social cohesion. Some of them are acutely vulnerable, others moderately so. Small states are neither among the wealthiest nor the poorest states. They are in a position to offset vulnerability in some cases, although their small size gives them less margin for coping than in larger states.

3. Small states' security starts at home. Social cohesion in most small states is a major resource which adds to resilience and lessens internal insecurity. Small states exhibit an enviable record of political stability. While this is to be welcomed there is no room for complacency since if order does break down in small states, conflict can quickly escalate beyond the survival of any particular regime to the survival of the core values of the society itself. Of most concern are economic threats linked to the globalisation of trade, investment, finance and production; environmental threats relating to the increased incidence and scale of natural disasters and the mounting damage of global warming; and threats to the fabric of society contained in the spread of transnational values. Expanding transnational activity has encouraged the growth of international crime which small states have found difficult to counter.

4. Small states are disadvantaged in international financial markets, finding it difficult to access private capital or concessional finance, to develop successful domestic capital markets or attract foreign direct investment. The implementation of the UR heralds the prospective ending of trade preferences which will put substantial pressure on many small states. The WTO is emerging as a major player in world affairs. Small states should therefore seek to become active in the

WTO, in responding to new regional economic arrangements and in facing prospective changes to the Lomé Convention. Advantages enjoyed by small states under the special protocols for sugar, bananas, and beef are likely to be eroded with damaging consequences for many of the Commonwealth's small states.

5. Small states are exposed to serious environmental risks such as natural disasters; vulnerability to sea-level rise, which threatens the physical existence of several small states and the viability of some others; marine pollution, which is increasing in scale and severity; deforestation, as a result of under-valuation of forest resources; desertification and soil erosion, caused by a combination of natural and human action; overfishing, by both small states and distant water fishing nations; and limited availability of fresh water.

6. Small states are not given any special recognition by the international system. While they have had some successes, the ability of small states to influence global affairs is limited. They should focus on specific issues of particular importance to them and where they may be able to shape outcomes.

7. Small states stand to gain from an international system in which regimes and institutions are central to the conduct of international affairs. They should help develop existing regimes, and promote others which directly contribute to their interests.

8. There is much small states can do themselves, collectively and individually, to ensure that most threats are met and overcome. They will continue to need external support to meet some threats especially through regional co-operation.

9. The UN is the most important international organisation for all small states. A properly working UN can do much to guarantee their security and advance their development. Small states should be active in the reform of the UN and seek to develop initiatives within it which can advance their interests.

10. The Commonwealth has contributed to the security and development of small states, acting as a global advocate of their interests. The part played by the Commonwealth in supporting small states is not matched by any other international organisation. Its programmes and interventions are to be welcomed and expanded. The Ministerial Group on Small States (MGSS) provides a suitable forum for the Commonwealth to keep a focus on small states' concerns.

Recommendations

11. The report's recommendations are grouped here and set out at the three levels at which they would be implemented: national, regional

and international. At each of the three levels, the recommendations are clustered sectorally, by economic, environmental and political issues. Many of the recommendations may be tackled at more than one level; regional co-operation would provide the key for success of most of the national and international-level recommendations concerning economic and environmental matters. Recommendations involving action by the Commonwealth are presented separately. The recommendations are mostly listed in order of appearance in the report, with numbers in brackets indicating the paragraphs where they are discussed.

National

Economic

12. The Uruguay Round agreements and other changes in the international system pose major transitional challenges. To benefit from them small states will need to re-orient their economies and diversify their production base (6.32).

13. In the field of trade policy, small states will need to introduce changes which stimulate and encourage the private sector and the government to identify and vigorously pursue new trading opportunities in the international system (6.33; 6.34).

14. Governments will need to introduce new measures to encourage optimum use of existing preferences under the Lomé Convention and to counter-balance the erosion of preferences for particular product groups. Product diversification and improved competitiveness must be a priority (6.34).

15. In respect of new issues in the Uruguay Round, small states should seek to develop trade and labour-intensive services; establish policy and institutional frameworks to attract foreign investment; and promote accession to the WTO by small states who are currently not members (6.35).

16. To fully exploit trading opportunities a proactive marketing policy by the government and the private sector through well-financed joint government–private sector programmes should be encouraged (6.39).

17. The mobilisation of domestic and foreign resources is essential. Governments should make a strong case to donors for assured flows of overseas development assistance during a transition phase in which they will need to introduce policies that encourage private investment, both foreign and domestic (6.42).

18. Small states that have yet to embark on reforms to liberalise the economy need to do so as a matter of urgency. Among measures to be

taken are changes in fiscal policy; acceleration of the pace of privatisation; the strengthening of the private sector; and seeking external support for transitional arrangements to cushion the cost of reforms (6.36; 6.46; 6.47).

19. An appropriate technology policy is vital. Small states should actively pursue initiatives at national, regional and international levels to develop technology which will enhance competitiveness and contribute to sustainable development (11.26).

Environmental

20. To reduce environmental vulnerabilities, small states need to implement strategies which address their most urgent environmental problems and integrate environmental considerations into the earliest stages of economic policy-making (8.50).

21. Small states should investigate and encourage innovative approaches to insurance in disaster-prone areas. Urgent consideration should be given to the introduction of an international insurance scheme for small states (8.56).

22. Market-based economic instruments should be encouraged and measures taken to apply such instruments to the tourism, energy, and fishing sectors as well as in fresh water provision (8.57).

23. Environmental thinking must be incorporated into macroeconomic management. 'Green national accounting' could be adopted. Measures must be taken to strengthen capacity in policy formation and implementation for biodiversity monitoring and assessment; sustainable forest management; improving water supply; combating desertification and drought; improving the surveillance and monitoring of exclusive economic zones (EEZs); and coastal zone management (8.58).

Political

24. Small state defence forces need to be configured to take on a variety of tasks. They should liaise closely with other government agencies and acquire a range of paramilitary skills (10.31).

25. Small states, while being mindful of the position of global powers, should seek security assistance from them in areas where there are overlapping interests, such as combating global crime, subject to safeguards concerning national sovereignty (10.32).

26. Efforts to develop information networks and, in securing international assistance and training, to enhance self-reliant defence efforts should remain a priority of small states (10.35).

27. Small states have a vested interest in ensuring their domestic regimes are politically acceptable, apart from the intrinsic value of maintaining democratic and accountable government in accordance with the principles of the Harare Declaration. They must ensure that mechanisms are in place to limit would-be dictators and to support democratic processes (10.32; 10.33).

Social

28. In tertiary education, small states should as an urgent priority undertake efforts to widen the curriculum, support technical training and, where possible, promote institutions to foster research and development (11.7).

29. In society as a whole, affirmative action should be taken to enable women and girls to access education, markets, credit, jobs, health care, legal services, decision-making fora, shelter, good sanitation and other resources. Human security requires policies of participation, empowerment and social integration. There is an urgent need for governments to create sufficient opportunities for productive employment and an onus on them to provide the appropriate environment for active citizenship to ensure that all groups are drawn into the conduct of public affairs (11.14; 11.17; 11.20).

Regional

Economic

30. Special regional development funds should be established and supported by international donors to identify emerging trade opportunities for goods and services produced in small states. They could also be used to facilitate the transfer of production technology, marketing skills and trade promotion (6.37).

31. Joint intergovernmental trade representation at the regional level would reduce costs in marketing and promotion for products common to small countries in that region (6.40).

32. Measures promoting trade and co-operation amongst a region's entrepreneurs should be encouraged as these are likely to have a positive impact on strengthening the private sector (6.47).

Environmental

33. Small states should be given appropriate regional assistance to identify and negotiate innovative sources of finance at the international level for environmental exploitation and conservation. Regional support

should also be sought to strengthen capacity in environmental policy formation and implementation (8.56; 8.58).

Political

34. Small states should supplement efforts to combat international crime at regional level with appropriate international action (10.36).

International

Economic

35. Small states should seek to persuade developed countries with which they have preferential trading arrangements of the benefits to small states of providing external support for economic reform programmes. Among measures that could be taken by developed countries are ones encouraging flows of foreign direct investment, increased imports of tropical products and more permissive 'rules of origin' (6.36).

36. Developed countries need to be reminded of their obligation to provide assistance to net-food importing countries should it be needed (6.38).

37. Bilateral and multilateral donor agencies should be urged to earmark and augment resources to support product and market diversification in small states (6.41).

38. In determining eligibility to concessional finance, bilateral and multilateral donors should recognise the special position of small states by taking account of a broader set of criteria other than per capita income (6.43).

39. International programmes of assistance should be directed at capacity-building, both in terms of infrastructure and the development of human capital. A combination of capital and technical assistance should be targeted towards meeting the goals and objectives of the Barbados Programme of Action (6.45).

Environmental

40. Small states should promote the full and effective implementation of the environmental conventions and agreements to which they are party (8.51).

41. In the light of the review of environmental issues at the Rio+5 Special Session of the UN General Assembly, small states need to take urgent action in a number of areas. Among them are promoting an effective agreement to reduce greenhouse gas emissions; ratification and implementation of the Convention on Desertification; seeking

support for measures to enhance the management of EEZs and promote sustainable fishing (e.g. through a possible Commonwealth Fisheries Protection Agreement); and accelerating implementation of the information network and technical assistance programmes agreed for small island developing states in the Barbados Programme of Action (8.52).

42. Small states should seek to persuade donor countries of the need to reverse the decline in overseas development assistance which has been a major constraint in implementing international environmental agreements. The Global Environment Facility should be adequately replenished and further streamlined to improve its operational scope and efficiency (8.53).

43. Small states should seek the establishment of a compensatory financing scheme within the UN system to provide funds for rehabilitation and reconstruction following natural disasters which affect them (8.54).

44. The international community, in close collaboration with small states, should develop effective instruments and arrangements concerning the transboundary movement of hazardous and nuclear waste (8.15; 8.51).

Political

45. Small states should use their number and in many cases their good example to strengthen multilateral co-operation as the basis for developing a more humane and equitable global order (12.31).

46. Small states should be proactive in promoting international law and international regimes in a number of areas. A study should be undertaken to determine which international regimes are of particular importance to small state security with a view to early ratification (12.32).

47. Small states must be supportive of reform of the UN and its emergence as the central institution of global governance. On the growing economic, environmental and humanitarian agendas, small states should ensure that they are at the centre of discussion and proposals for reform (12.33).

Commonwealth

Economic

48. Commonwealth Ministers are requested to urge the World Bank and the Inter-American Development Bank to review their graduation policies and establish multiple criteria, which take into account the

special vulnerablities and costs of its smallest borrowing members (6.43).

49. To assist international consideration of the special problems of small states and to improve their eligibility for concessional finance, the development of a robust vulnerability index is essential and should receive the highest priority in the Commonwealth Secretariat (6.44).

Environmental

50. The Commonwealth should play an active role in the review of the Barbados Programme of Action scheduled for 1999 (8.52).

51. Commonwealth and non-Commonwealth donors are urged to provide support for the innovative and exemplary Iwokrama International Rainforest Programme in Guyana (8.59).

Political

52. In recognition of the special role the Commonwealth can play in combating international crime, priority should be given by the Commonwealth Secretariat to practical measures to help smail states combat drug trafficking and money laundering at national, regional and international levels (10.37).

53. We recommend that Commonwealth small states not permanently present at the UN should examine the benefit of joining the Joint Office (12.33).

54. The Commonwealth is well placed to promote good governance and, where necessary, provide practical advice to small states to prevent or resolve conflict as an addition to other measures being undertaken (11.23).

Social

55. Distance learning is an approach which should be encouraged and supported, where necessary, with funds and support from other Commonwealth states (11.8).

Institutional

56. There is a need to strengthen present arrangements within the Commonwealth Secretariat to co-ordinate programmes of assistance to small states, including developing relations with non-governmental organisations (12.34).

Commonwealth small states

Of Commonwealth's 54 members, 32 are classified as small states

South Pacific

Fiji
Kiribati
Nauru
Papua New Guinea
Samoa
Solomon Islands
Tonga
Tuvalu
Vanuatu

Europe

Cyprus
Malta

Asia

Brunei Darussalam
Maldives

Africa

Botswana
The Gambia
Lesotho
Mauritius
Namibia
Seychelles
Swaziland

Caribbean

Antigua and Barbuda
The Bahamas
Barbados
Belize
Dominica
Grenada
Guyana
Jamaica
St Kitts and Nevis
St Lucia
St Vincent
Trinidad and Tobago

Map source: ComSec/Maps-in-Minutes

1

Introduction

Terms of Reference

1.1 This study is the result of a mandate given to the Commonwealth Secretariat by the Commonwealth Ministerial Group on Small States at its meeting in Auckland, New Zealand, in November 1995. The mandate followed from earlier discussions about the problems and special needs of small states, which had identified challenges to small states in a number of areas including the environment, global trade and security. Ministers called for an updating of the report, *Vulnerability: Small States in the Global Society*, prepared by the Commonwealth Consultative Group in 1985, and requested that in reviewing the security concerns of small states the multi-dimensional nature of security be kept fully in view.

1.2 The 1985 *Vulnerability* report set out the characteristics of small states and then analysed various factors which suggested small states functioned at a disadvantage compared to larger states. It argued that small states were inherently vulnerable and that the international community had obligations to ensure their survival and prosperity. Much of the *Vulnerability* report was concerned with military and political security against external threats reflecting the interests in small states which had been kindled by the invasion of Grenada in 1983. But the report also considered other factors which threatened small states including the vagaries of the world economy and the internal social cohesiveness of states. Stress was laid on policies to secure economic growth and to advance small states' interests in the international system through effective diplomacy. The report ended with a lengthy list of recommendations for the states themselves and for the Commonwealth.

1.3 In reviewing the *Vulnerability* report the Secretariat concluded that it would need to be substantially rewritten to take account of all major developments since 1985. These included the widespread adoption of development strategies which assign a central role to market forces; the systemic changes in the international trading system brought about by the Uruguay Round; regionalisation of the global economy with the emergence of 'mega-economic spaces' such as the Asian Pacific Economic Co-operation forum (APEC), the European

1

Union/European Economic Area and the North American Free Trade Agreement (NAFTA); declining resource flows to small states; possibly disastrous consequences for small states as a result of global warming and climate change, and environmental fragility; new threats to security, including vulnerability to criminal activities such as money laundering, and transboundary movement of hazardous waste and nuclear material; and the growing importance of gender-related issues in the development process.

The Insecurity of Small States

1.4 The *Vulnerability* report was framed and written in a world order largely set by the Cold War. The predominant themes were geopolitical and some of the most worrying threats for small states derived from geopolitical rivalry. The early 1980s were a period in which the Cold War intensified and superpower intervention in many regions of the world increased significantly. The effects were felt by small states in a number of ways, ranging from direct intervention in the Caribbean to the spread of Cold War strategic thinking in the South Pacific. Attention shifted from the economic and development difficulties of small states to the problems of independence and security in an insecure world. The popular conception of 'small is beautiful' became qualified by an understanding in the wake of Grenada that 'small is dangerous' and 'small is vulnerable'.

1.5 The shift in perception was marked by a flurry of interest in small states. A number of studies appeared addressing their problems. In virtually every one the insecurity of small states was acknowledged to be a product not only of international competition and relative weakness but also of economic dependence and political indifference by the international community. There was also a recognition that small states' security problems were multi-dimensional and required a more comprehensive approach than for many larger states; and that small states themselves would need to do more than they had in the past to address security questions.

1.6 These ideas infuse the *Vulnerability* report which was premised on two core insights: (1) that security and development are interrelated and (2) that threats to security have internal as well as external origins. The analysis was comprehensive. The characteristics of smallness were set out along with the vulnerabilities of small states. In the chapters on threats, the main external and internal threats faced by small states were discussed in detail. The policy dimension was a particular feature of the report. Proposals were made under a number of headings: strengthening national defence capability; underpinning economic growth; promoting internal cohesion; diplomacy and foreign policy management; and the international response. The report concluded by identifying eight arenas for action and made 79 specific recommendations which are appended as an Annex to this report.

1.7 Much of the analysis and many of the recommendations remain relevant today. At the same time, it is clear that the ending of the Cold War has changed significantly the context in which small states operate. The structure of the international system has fragmented so that it is no longer possible to speak meaningfully in political terms of a First World and a Third World or to be as confident of significantly different objectives between the advanced industrialised economies of the North and the developing countries of the South. International organisations, too, have had to adapt to changing conditions and some, such as the International Monetary Fund (IMF), the World Bank and the recently created World Trade Organisation (WTO), have become significant world players setting the agenda and pace of global change. The United Nations, freed from the constraints of the Cold War, has an opportunity to become the focus of a new system of international governance of benefit to all humankind. However, its effectiveness to date has been limited and small states, along with other states, have become engaged in relations with an increasing number of international actors.

1.8 Added to this is the uncertainty of the strategic landscape. The collapse of the Soviet Union has left only the United States as a superpower. Its willingness to take on a different global role than before was announced by President Bush in his call for a 'New International Order' made at the time of the Gulf War. But in practice there has been uncertainty and unpredictability surrounding the exercise of leadership by the US across the board and its undoubted military strength has been affected by the realisation that military power has changed in importance in international affairs. Many of the issues troubling the world today are not open to military solution: power is more diffuse and threats now take a multitude of forms which, with the exception of some war-torn regions, are essentially non-military in character. Among them are poverty at home and abroad; resource shortages and environmental hazards; and drug trafficking and international crime, to name but a few.

1.9 The new multipolar system which appears in the making is fed by seemingly contradictory impulses: on the one hand the embrace of globalisation and on the other the growth of regionalism. Globalisation is most easily comprehended as a process of accelerating interdependence which has at its core the liberalisation of trade, the deregulation of financial markets, the spread of transnational production of goods and services, and the development of new technologies, particularly information technology. There are also cultural elements to the phenomena associated with the diffusion of consumerist values, environmental concerns focused on the protection of seas and habitat, and political issues to do with the effectiveness of the state. Indeed, states now have to recognise the power not only of other states and international organisations, but also of a range of other actors from impersonal foreign exchange markets through transnational firms to individual terrorist and criminal activity.

1.10 Contrary to this is the prospective strengthening of the state through regionalism. The image of a multipolar world is based on emerging blocs of states seeking competitive advantage in the global economy through closer economic and political integration. This is weakening existing state boundaries and prefiguring the emergence of new ones. While it is easy to see the leading players in this process in Europe, North America and Asia it is still too early to determine whether this will create new superpowers and a new centralised balance of power or result in a more decentralised system structure. However, the processes already under way are widening the asymmetries of power in the international system.

1.11 The world has also become more complex in other ways. The ideological division between capitalism and communism may have gone but new divisions have opened between states and peoples. Ethnic tensions and religious fundamentalism have led to conflicts within and between states in various parts of the world, increasing suffering and contributing to an ever mounting flow of refugees. In some cases states have collapsed and others have been put under strain as they have tried to cope with AIDS and drugs. The programmes of structural adjustment which have been negotiated between such states and the international financial institutions (IFIs) and major donors have met with some success, but in other cases they have increased inequality and in some instances led to political turmoil and social unrest.

1.12 In short, small states face a more uncertain and more unstable world than they did a decade ago. So far, all Commonwealth small states have managed to survive and some even to thrive. But the stresses are real enough and in many instances not directly of their own making. The environment can be cited as a particular case where external factors play a significant part in increasing risk. The international community has acknowledged that small island developing states (SIDS) are especially vulnerable, but has failed to put in place the measures or provide the resources which would significantly diminish the threats to which they are exposed. Another set of threats arise from the international economy. Globalisation may provide some benefits but it could also lead to the marginalisation and impoverishment of small states, particularly those that are the least developed and least capable of making the changes needed to take advantage of new opportunities.

1.13 Small states cannot evade their own responsibilities for managing change. They can and have done much to improve their relative security at national and regional levels. But in the end it is difficult to escape the conclusion that it is the international level which is decisive in setting the structure within which small states have to act and determining the agenda to which they must respond. The *Vulnerability* report expressed this in its stress on 'a compelling obligation' by the international community to recognise the 'special vulnerabilities and special needs' of small states and a warning that if these are not addressed 'the prospects for small states could become serious'. Some recognition has been given by the international community to small states with the Commonwealth noticeably to the fore. But much remains to be done and if small states no longer face the same level of geopolitical threat as they did in the mid-1980s, they face even greater economic and environmental threats at the end of the 1990s. The ways in which small states are insecure may have changed, but the fact of their vulnerability remains.

1.14 It can, however, be lessened. Most Commonwealth small states have a positive track record in maintaining democracy and scoring significant advances in the economic and social well-being of their people in the last decade. They have internal strengths which can be harnessed to further improve human development. They have accumulated considerable experience in international affairs and have some successes behind them. It is in recognition of this and our belief that small states can, with the support of the international community, overcome the difficulties they face that we have entitled this report, *A Future for Small States: Overcoming Vulnerability*. Small states have much to offer the world and with the right policies and help from international organisations like the Commonwealth they can be contributors to global security and development.

The Structure of the Report

1.15 The report presented here examines the way such changes have affected the fortunes of Commonwealth small states. It does not seek to revisit ground previously covered in the *Vulnerability* report but to build on its pioneering and insightful analysis by including new subjects and new material. This has shifted the balance of the report toward economic and environmental issues. At the same time, care has also been taken to update and review the type of security concerns which were very much at the heart of the previous report. The current report is therefore at one and the same time a new report, a revised report and an updated report. Insofar as any one study can be it also seeks to be comprehensive in its treatment of the now very broad security concerns of small states, although necessarily it cannot be exhaustive of all the issues they have to face.

1.16 The report proceeds as follows:

Chapter 2 defines smallness and identifies the general characteristics which bear on the security of small states. It then examines the concept of vulnerability and its close association with small size.

Chapter 3 establishes the need for a multi-dimensional approach to identifying threats to small states. It then lists the threats that small states typically face in various political, economic, social and environmental dimensions.

Chapter 4 looks at the economic consequences of being small and exposes the economic disadvantages which small states have compared to larger states.

Chapter 5 examines the changing world economic order by setting out some of the important effects that globalisation and regionalisation have had on small states and some of the ways small states can hope to meet the challenges and profit from the opportunities provided by these twin developments.

Chapter 6 looks at ways in which small states can cope with some of the major economic issues of global and regional change which bear immediately and directly upon them. It sets out several strategies which small states may wish to adopt internationally to maintain or improve their position.

Chapter 7 examines the vulnerability of small states from an environmental perspective. It identifies external and internal risks and raises the issue of the sustainable development of small states.

Chapter 8 reviews some of the ways small states cope with environmental challenges. It examines the special problems which confront small island developing states and highlights the linkage between the environment and the economy. The proposition is that small states are especially sensitive to environmental issues and must be particularly aware of a holistic approach to managing the environment if natural resources are to be husbanded and economic well-being maintained.

Chapter 9 focuses largely, but not exclusively, on the military and political dimensions of security. It discusses the wide variety of threats to which small states have been exposed in differing regional environments and identifies the major threats to small states that have arisen in the last ten years.

Chapter 10 examines the policies open to small states to enhance their security through self-help and through the involvement of other powers. It reviews the national capabilities of states and looks at ways these can be improved internally and bilaterally as well as through close co-operation with regional institutions.

Chapter 11 looks at the issue of national capacity. It explores ways in which improvements to the human capacity of small states can underpin economic growth and social welfare, improving the cohesion of a state and its prospects for sustainable development.

Chapter 12 discusses the international institutional context in which small states conduct diplomacy. It sets out the importance to them of several international organisations and elaborates initiatives they have and may wish to take, including within the Commonwealth.

2

Smallness and Vulnerability

2.1 There have always been small states in the international system. In some periods they have been the norm rather than the exception and have set the pattern of relations between states. In the current state system small states tend to be overlooked. This arises from the enormous disparities of power between states in the present system compared to previous systems. Such disparities expose them to threats they find difficult to counter and make them vulnerable to systemic shocks which they cannot control. At the same time it is important to recognise that subject to differing definitions of 'what is small', small states constitute between a quarter to half the number of sovereign states in the current international system. But they lack influence and this is particularly the case for the smallest among them. These have varied profiles but they also hold much in common. This chapter examines these issues identifying which states are 'small', why they are more similar than dissimilar to each other, and why they remain vulnerable.

Definition

2.2 No wholly agreed definition of a small state presently exists. Any definition is therefore to some degree arbitrary, although it may be less so if two considerations are borne in mind. First, economists have demonstrated that for small countries a high correlation exists between population and other measures of economic size such as total GNP and total land area, confirming that in economic analysis it is reasonable to define small states by population criterion alone. Second, that the concept of smallness, being relative, has continually undergone revision, reflecting the character of the international system at the time. Since the Second World War more than a hundred states have been created and the 89 countries with a population of five million or less are now just short of a numerical majority in the international system, leading to the need to distinguish within this broad category the particular interests of the smallest members.

2.3 In practice this has been achieved by defining a small state as one with a population of around one million or less. This was taken as the defining criterion in the 1985 *Vulnerability* report and has stood the test of time very well. It is familiar and it is widely used. At the same time world population has increased and a relative upward adjustment of population figures is necessary to take account of this fact. A revised upper limit of 1.5 million is taken as the new cut-off point. On current population figures there are 49 independent states with populations of 1.5 million or below, 28 of which are in the Commonwealth and 42 in the developing world.

2.4 An additional consideration is the importance of region. The *Vulnerability* report argued that the particular circumstances of the Caribbean, the South Pacific and Southern Africa warranted the inclusion of Jamaica, Papua New Guinea, and Lesotho because they shared many physical and economic characteristics with all the small states of their region. That conclusion still holds with the further addition of Namibia which has since joined the Commonwealth. The countries covered in the study are given in Table 2.1.

The Characteristics of Small States

2.5 While small states are very different from each other it is possible to identify certain features which many of the small states identified in Table 2.1 hold in common and which bear directly on their security. These have been identified as openness, insularity or 'enclaveness', resilience, weakness and dependence (Sutton & Payne, 1993). They can be positive as well as negative, providing a different balance of advantage or disadvantage to any individual state depending on the degree and mix of the various elements.

2.6 **Openness** is traditionally associated with the external focus of the economy in which international trade assumes greater significance than in larger states and in which diversification of production is markedly less. But it also has significant political and cultural manifestations. The former is witnessed in the penetrability of the political system, where a relatively greater shortage of managerial and technical capabilities allows for higher levels of expatriate staffing and increased reliance on external threat assessment than would be the case in most states. The latter is seen in the greater propensity to look outward and migrate than is the case in many other countries, combined with a readiness to adopt foreign cultural norms which encourages the erosion of values and identity. While this has obvious negative effects, there can also be positive benefits in the higher levels of sensitivity in such countries to changes in the international system which allow for adaptation and innovation. Openness stimulates competition and permits small states to exploit new opportunities in the emerging global economy provided by the mobility of international finance.

9

Table 2.1 Population of Small* Developing States Included in the Study

	Population (1995)
Caribbean	
Antigua and Barbuda	65,000
The Bahamas	276,000
Barbados	261,000
Belize	216,000
Dominica	73,000
Grenada	91,000
Guyana	835,000
St Kitts and Nevis	41,000
St Lucia	158,000
St Vincent and the Grenadines	111,000
Suriname	410,000
Trinidad and Tobago	1,287,000
Jamaica	2,522,000
South Pacific	
Fiji	775,000
Kiribati	79,000
Micronesia	107,000
Marshall Islands	56,000
Nauru	8,000
Palau	16,000
Samoa	165,000
Solomon Islands	375,000
Tonga	104,000
Tuvalu	11,000
Vanuatu	169,000
Papua New Guinea	4,302,000
Africa	
Botswana	1,450,000
Cape Verde	380,000
Djibouti	634,000
Equatorial Guinea	400,000
Gabon	1,077,000
The Gambia	1,113,000
Guinea-Bissau	1,070,000
Namibia	1,545,000
Sao Tome e Principe	129,000
Swaziland	900,000
Lesotho	1,980,000
Indian Ocean	
Comoros	499,000
Maldives	253,000
Mauritius	1,128,000
Seychelles	74,000
Mediterrranean	
Cyprus	734,000
Malta	372,000
Middle East	
Bahrain	548,000
Qatar	642,000
Asia	
Brunei Darussalam	285,000

*Member countries of the Commonwealth are shown in **bold**.

Source: Commonwealth Secretariat, *Small States: Economic Review and Basic Statistics* (1997).

2.7 **Insularity** is especially associated with small states. Thirty-two small states are islands and when the islands are also small much of life is conditioned by an awareness of insularity. This is often manifest in a close association with a sense of place which gives preference to individual identity over collective solidarity, making co-operation between islands problematic and secession an ever-present possibility. Other common characteristics are remoteness, which has considerable economic and administrative costs, environmental precariousness, which is seen in the dangers of frequent natural disasters, and acute indefensibility posed by the problems of meeting a multitude of potential or actual threats from the sea with limited resources. At the same time many island states have benefited from the UN Convention on the Law of the Sea (UNCLOS) which gives them rights to resource-rich Exclusive Economic Zones (EEZs) which extend over tens of thousands of square kilometres and promise considerable economic benefits in years to come. Many are also well situated geographically and climatically to benefit from the fast-growing tourist market.

2.8 **Resilience** is a property associated with the political and social systems of small states. There is a strong measure of institutional coherence in many small states which has encouraged constitutional development and the spread of democracy. Small states are more likely to be democratic than large states, irrespective of levels of economic development. This suggests a greater measure of political consensus and of social cohesion than applies in larger societies. The predominant political culture is one of 'concerted political harmony' which sees incremental change as the most effective way to promote political legitimacy and deliver efficient administration. In consequence, and in comparison to other states, small states exhibit an enviable record of political stability. Nevertheless, political order does, on occasion, break down and examples of small states with repressive political systems can be found. However, the comparative rarity of such cases confirms the general rule: the political regimes of small states tend to be pragmatic and robust, able to withstand significant challenges which larger states would find difficult to meet. They are also significantly better performers in delivering human development than larger states, with many of them to be found in the upper ranks of the listings for the developing world set out in the United Nations Development Programme's Human Development Index.

2.9 **Weakness** derives from an international system based largely or in part on power. Small states have very low military capabilities and cannot do much individually to defend themselves from aggression. Accordingly, they must rely more than other states do on the international system to maintain their security. This provides three alternative strategies at the present time: (1) neutrality; (2) alliance with the super-power or one or more of the major powers and/or regional powers; (3) collective security, in a universal and/or regional organisation. Neutrality is a difficult legal status to gain and sustain and is usually related to exceptional conditions pertaining to the state. Alliances are treated with caution since the asymmetry of power between the partners introduces greater uncertainty and risk for the smaller state than the larger. Nevertheless, many small states have sought informal under-standings on their security with major powers or regional powers to provide them with an 'umbrella' under which their survival in the face of extreme threats can be assured. Finally, while the established guarantee of security for a small state is a universal collective security system prepared to resist aggression on their behalf, an alternative route at present is through various regional arrangements in which the small state can hope to have its particular security needs identified and accepted.

2.10 **Dependence** is a general condition affecting many developing countries. For small states, and particularly the smallest among them, it is a way of life. This has led to their orientation being more often outward than inward, especially in the economic sector, where it is most clearly evident in their reliance on invisible income from remittances and tourism, their relatively greater levels of official development assistance (ODA) per capita than in larger states, and in their need to maintain preferential trading arrangements to ensure the continuing access of their products to metropolitan markets. These features have rendered small states vulnerable to adverse developments in the economy, domestic politics and foreign policy of the larger states and great powers with which they have had close ties. At the same time, it is important to note that dependence is not a static concept and that changes in the international system can provide new opportunities for both sets of partners from which each can benefit, as in the promotion of offshore financial services or greater awareness of the needs of environmental protection.

2.11 These characteristics are interrelated and provide an overview of the most important elements of security for the majority of small states. None of them individually are exclusive to small states, but collectively they provide insights into why the security of small states is different in degree rather than in kind to larger states. All of them will be examined at greater length elsewhere in the study with particular reference to three dimensions: the economic, the environmental and the political. In each dimension small states will have to meet and overcome the constraints which have been sketched out if they are to maintain or advance their security. It is not, however, entirely a negative story. Many small states possess significant advantages. They have resilient political structures, good social capital, large EEZs and an openness to the outside world which allows them to adapt to changed circumstances. This provides them with the opportunity to fashion policies which minimise disadvantage and maximise potential. The record of success in small states shows they can achieve levels of security and development above the average. While small states remain vulnerable, they do not remain helpless.

The Concept of Vulnerability

2.12 To be vulnerable is to be especially susceptible to risk of harm. Since all societies are subject to risk, all societies are vulnerable. What makes vulnerability a focus of concern is that some societies are more at risk than others. The baseline for comparison can be societies in general or some comparator group of societies. In the current context the vulnerability of small states is a subject of concern because of the presumption that small states are more at risk than states in general or more at risk than 'big' states. This was a proposition advanced in the *Vulnerability* report which referred to 'the inherent vulnerability of small states' in the contemporary international system due to their limited human resource base and low economic capacity to meet threats.

2.13 What is being addressed here is the significance of the internal properties of a country. A given state, society or ecosystem may be subject to many threats and exposed to many risks but may have the ability to resist them or, if it cannot, it may have the ability to return to a prior path of social, environmental, economic and political development, i.e. to reconstruct itself without major disruption. The concept of vulnerability therefore has to take into account the ability of a country to respond to risk. At the same time it is also clear that vulnerability is increased if a country is exposed to high levels of threat and multiple sources of risk. The important determinant here will be the external environment in which it is located as some areas of the world are more inhospitable or more prone to conflict and turmoil than are others.

2.14 Vulnerability is thus the consequence of the interaction of two sets of factors: (1) the incidence and intensity of risk and threat and (2) the ability to withstand risks and threats (resistance) and to 'bounce back' from their consequences (resilience). A country may therefore be highly vulnerable in the narrow sense, i.e. be especially at risk, but may not be vulnerable because of its ability to resist the risk. An example might be a country especially at risk from hurricanes, but which has high standards of building such that buildings damage and risks to human life are minimised. In the same way, a country may be at risk from hurricanes but may have a well-functioning administrative procedure for coping with the consequences, allowing it to provide relief and rehabilitation without massive upheaval. Somewhat differently a country may be at risk from drug traffickers or mercenaries but have in place such a sure system of detection and such a draconian range of penalties that it is not threatened by them. One obvious implication of this understanding of vulnerability is that societies that are poor in human and economic resources are likely to be vulnerable relative to any given risk they face. They will tend not to have the ability to resist or reconstruct rapidly. Equally it follows that countries which can anticipate threats but do little to deter them are more at risk than those that do take appropriate action.

2.15 Vulnerability thus always implies susceptibility to something and by something. Physical vulnerability will tend to relate to the risks faced by ecological systems and by the human-made environment to climatic events, other natural disasters (such as earthquakes) and to human-made pollution. Economic vulnerability will refer to the susceptibility of economic sectors, such as agriculture, and of the economy as a whole, to both internal and external risks. Social vulnerability relates to the exposure of individuals and social groups to risks of climatic events (hurricanes, sea-level rise etc.), disease, economic events (such as sudden increases in the price of imports or falls in the price of exports) and political events (such as ethnic conflict and the breakdown of law and order). Political vulnerability relates to threats to territorial integrity, core values and internal cohesion from forces outside and inside the state. The extent to which susceptibility becomes vulnerability depends on the ability of the receiving agents to respond to risk by resistance (including deterrence) and resilience.

Size and Vulnerability

2.16 Given that resilience has been identified as a feature of many small states their vulnerability, in some respects, is correspondingly reduced. At the same time it is clear that resistance to threats is governed by size, especially when one considers the number and magnitude of risks and threats faced by small states. Some small states will face high levels of risks/threats which they will be unable to resist: they will be acutely vulnerable to harm. Others will face lower levels of risks/threats which they can manage with difficulty but without irreparable harm: they will be moderately vulnerable. Finally some will face minimal threats or be sufficiently resistant to them to avoid significant harm: they remain inherently vulnerable even though they are not significantly at risk.

2.17 What most will have in common, however, is a susceptibility to risks and threats set at a relatively lower threshold than for larger states. This is the product of size. It is the consequence of the interrelationship between the characteristics of small states identified earlier and while it has political and environmental dimensions, it is most readily identifiable in the economy. Pioneering work by Briguglio (1995) demonstrated a relationship between economic vulnerabilities and SIDS which disadvantaged them but which was insufficiently recognised by the international community in assessing the development needs of such states. Preliminary work on a composite vulnerability index for all small states has been undertaken by the Commonwealth Secretariat. That work appears to confirm that Briguglio's finding is applicable to all small states and highlights the need to adjust the per capita income figures for small states in a downward direction to take their vulnerabilities into account. Additional studies by the Secretariat are currently underway to refine the index with the example of the widely-used Human Development Index very much in mind. While the findings from these studies are at the moment tentative they do verify what has been argued in the *Vulnerability* report and elsewhere: that small states face external constraints, risks and threats that impact on them to a degree both qualitatively and quantitatively different from other states, making them especially vulnerable.

3

The Threat Scenario

3.1 The end of the Cold War has introduced new uncertainties into international relations, while globalisation has introduced new threats and opportunities for all states. For small states, the changes introduced have impacted on them largely in terms of degree rather than kind. That is, the threats they have faced have not been specific to them, although it is argued that in some cases they have impacted on them with greater force than for many other states. The number of threats have also multiplied and changed their relative weighting, with economic and environmental threats assuming greater significance in the security agendas of small states. This, in turn, implies a broader definition of security than existed during the Cold War. This chapter offers such a definition and then sets out the range of security threats typically, but not exclusively, facing small states.

The Definition of Threat and National Security

3.2 The 1985 *Vulnerability* report provided a working definition of national security as 'the absence of threat to the capacity to govern, protect, preserve and advance the state and its peoples consistent with the principle of respect for the sovereignty and territorial integrity of other states'. While reservations were expressed as to the correctness of the definition, particularly with respect to 'peoples', this definition has the merit of pointing out the acute vulnerability of small states insofar as in specifying the 'absence of threat' it makes the point that the absolute security of a small state can, in the last resort, only be guaranteed when there is no threat at all. At the same time, it is also clear that all states are to some measure relatively insecure. The degree of security available to small states is thus the important element to determine. It is reasonable to infer that this will be much less in small states than in large states, but not entirely absent.

3.3 Another issue arising from the definition in the *Vulnerability* report is the origin of the definition. It is clearly derived from the classic literature on the need to preserve and protect the core values of a nation. Again this has merit, but does not sufficiently capture the expanding domain of security in the post-Cold War world. Security now embraces human, economic and environmental dimensions and involves actors other than the state. Accordingly, a wider definition of threat is required, particularly as the report drew attention to the salience of economic threats from a variety of governmental and non-governmental sources.

3.4 The working definition of threat is taken from Ullman (1983): 'A threat to national security is an action or a sequence of events that (1) threatens drastically and over a relatively brief period of time to degrade the quality of life for the inhabitants of a state, or (2) threatens significantly to narrow the range of policy choices available to a state or to private non-governmental entities (persons, groups, corporations) within the state'. This definition incorporates economic and environmental concerns, a range of actors, and highlights vulnerability. It is not a definition 'mainstream' security theorists would embrace but it is essential in specifying the particular circumstances facing small states.

3.5 Finally, the definition in the *Vulnerability* report rightly draws attention to the obligation of a state to meet threats and advance interests consistent with respect for the purposes and principles of the UN Charter. These remain the cornerstone of the international system. At the same time the norms, rights and duties of states have expanded in recent years to take account of growing interdependence. In turn, this has emphasised the importance of international regimes, global governance and above all international law. These provide important elements of security for small states and need to be nurtured by them.

3.6 To give expression to the above points the new working definition of security is therefore 'the ability to manage threats to the capacity to govern, protect, preserve and advance the state and its people consistent with the principles of international law'. Threats are understood as including vulnerabilities as set out in 3.4. It is this consideration which is all important and distinguishes the high level of insecurity of small states as against larger ones.

The Range of Security Threats to Small States

3.7 The *Vulnerability* report identified three major categories of threats to security: threats to territorial security; threats to political security; and threats to economic security. These remain, although the experience since 1985 suggests some new threats have arisen or acquired prominence, particularly in relation to the environment and to social cohesion.

Threats to territorial security

3.8 The military threats included direct aggression and/or invasion by forces of another state or other agencies; establishment of foreign bases; and island states and secession. The incidence of these threats have been low. Since 1985, small states, with the significant exception of Kuwait, have not been prey to other states. At the same time the risk remains, particularly in respect of secession where new developments related to globalisation and to governance provide opportunity and grievance.

3.9 Non-military threats have mushroomed. Piracy, international criminal conspiracy and trespass of exclusive economic zones have all increased world-wide. The major threat has come from the drug trade but the other threats remain pertinent elsewhere and need to be addressed, particularly in SIDS.

Threats to political security

3.10 These threats remain imprecise. As identified in the *Vulnerability* report they include political and economic pressure for policy changes exercised by large states; destabilisation or subversion attempts resulting from political objectives of larger powers, or externally-based dissidents; spill-over effects of policy changes in member countries of a region; adverse impact of hostile or unsympathetic reporting by foreign media; and attempts at extra-territorial jurisdiction.

3.11 The identification of such threats and their incidence arise directly from an international politics based on national interest and power. Insofar as these remain important determinants of foreign policy they are endemic to the system. However, post-Cold War changes suggest a changing agenda and incidence of risk. The privileging of geo-economics in the interests of the great powers provides a situation where competition among them is increasingly based on economic criteria not geo-political rivalry. In this situation the principal concerns of small states are not the unwanted attentions of the great powers but the fear of being marginalised. Whilst military instruments continue to be used, economic measures are being increasingly applied by great powers to achieve their ends.

3.12 The acceleration of interdependence in the last decade also has had the effect of further blurring the distinction between foreign and domestic policy. It is now widely accepted that a distinction between the two is difficult to sustain and the emergence of issues such as human rights to international prominence have identified strong linkages between the internal politics of states and the international system. This points to the need to identify one additional political feature omitted from the *Vulnerability* report except by inference: regime instability as a trigger for intervention directed at changing or preserving the structure of political authority. The need to do so arises from the broader definition of threat adopted here. It also reflects the fact that most analyses of 'crises' in small states, especially those leading to intervention, identify internal threats to the political regime as the most significant precipitating factor.

3.13 Small states continue to be exposed to the whole range of political threats. At the same time changes within the international system have reduced the number of direct threats and increased the number of indirect threats. The general effect has been to increase the political insecurity of small states, particularly since such threats are nebulous and difficult to respond to in any precise way.

Threats to economic security

3.14 Economic threats are closely linked to the vulnerabilities of small states. As with many political threats it is difficult to identify when an economic threat begins and ends, how much it is latent or manifest, and how general or specific its effect will be. Nevertheless, there is a widespread consensus among the majority of leaders of small states that economic threats have increased in significance in recent years to the point where they constitute the single largest category of threats with the potential to impose the most harm.

3.15 Most of these fears pertain to the effects of globalisation and the belief that small, less developed states will be at a particular disadvantage. But it also corresponds to the increased use of economic policy in the foreign policies of states and to the growth of intergovernmental and transnational economic activity in the international system. The move to a volatile global economic system in which competition and bargaining constitute the essential framework within which policy is developed exposes the weakness of small states in a number of areas, earlier identified as economic hazards in the *Vulnerability* report. In particular, those associated with the exercise of undue political and economic influence by foreign business interests and an inadequate capacity to monitor and police EEZs can be flagged.

3.16 Another set of threats which have acquired prominence relate to the growth of money laundering and other economic crimes which impact negatively on the economy and undermine the financial integrity of the state. The removal of exchange and capital controls in recent years has led to a phenomenal growth in financial markets with daily global foreign exchange market turnover reaching an average of US$ 1,190 billion in early 1995. The growth of these markets is contributing to globalisation and is providing opportunities for many countries to establish offshore centres which offer a range of legitimate financial services. Among the more active in developing such centres have been small states and dependent territories which provide a variety of banking, insurance and business services in conditions of strict confidentiality. While such facilities are attractive to many corporations in the course of their business activities they also offer opportunities for tax evasion and for international criminals to launder money.

3.17 Money laundering is the process by which the proceeds of criminal activities such as drug trafficking, arms trafficking, financial fraud and organised crime are turned into apparently legitimate resources. The scope and scale of such activities have grown and now reach some US$ 500 billion globally each year. In small states, more than other states, the inflows and outflows of laundered money can have serious effects including distorting macroeconomic policy formation and implementation; introducing elements of volatility and imbalance into exchange rates; and compromising legitimate institutions in the financial sector leading to loss of financial confidence in the state by local savers as well as by international companies and institutions. Unchecked, money laundering increases the economic and financial power of international criminal syndicates, undermining democratic systems and respect for the rule of law through corruption, violence and undue influence in government. The adoption of effective measures to curb money laundering, while retaining the benefits of deregulated financial services, is a complex and politically sensitive subject which requires careful consideration.

3.18 However, by far the greatest threat is that of economic exclusion. The architecture of the new economic order is being built without the effective participation of small states. There is a formidable asymmetry of power, attention and representation within international organisations and agencies dealing primarily with economic issues. The lobbying networks which have grown to serve them serve those who can command the financial resources or the political muscle to get their views heard. Small states have little to offer individually in such an arena in which economic sovereignty is seen as simply something to trade, not to preserve. The consequences are far reaching, demanding a different strategy of response and a wider vision of threats than set out in the *Vulnerability* report.

Environmental threats

3.19 The single greatest threat to a small state is a natural disaster. They include cyclone, drought, desertification, earthquake, flood, hurricane, landslide, storm, tsunami, typhoon and volcano. Their number have significantly increased in frequency and magnitude over the last thirty years. Their impact is massive and affects not only infrastructure but also residential and commercial property on land and water, human health and life, transport, agriculture, livestock and business activities generally. The cost of recovery from such disasters adds to public expenditure and government indebtedness, both domestic and foreign as overseas financial assistance is often required. The cumulative effect of a series of disasters year on year can be especially debilitating, particularly for the poor and socially disadvantaged who suffer the most.

3.20 Other threats are not so dramatic but remain significant in their effects. They include plant and animal diseases which often relate to past practices of land use and animal husbandry and have caused serious damage to local ecosystems as well as putting the welfare of farmers and pastoralists at risk. There is also the question of human health. Small states find it difficult to provide the infrastructure and expertise to deliver a comprehensive range of health services and among the least developed there is a serious underprovision of medical personnel and hospital facilities. Access to safe water supplies is also unacceptably low in some states and AIDS remains an important issue in several countries where the rates of infection are particularly high and the capacity to screen and to respond to situations difficult.

3.21 While there is little that can be directly done to avoid some of these threats others are the product of human action and therefore can be controlled. The most serious are the adverse implications of climate change and sea-level rise due to global warming. Small island states are particularly at risk and as with natural disasters the effects are numerous and costly. With increasing scientific evidence that human activities are having a discernible influence on the world's climate, the need for an agreement, under the 1992 Convention on Climate Change, on significant reductions in greenhouse gas emissions has become more urgent. Since a certain degree of sea-level rise is in any case inevitable due to past emissions, the most vulnerable small islands will have to start protecting themselves against, and adapting to, its impacts, with assistance from the international community.

3.22 Coastal, marine and forest resources have also come under threat. Much of this is related to opportunities for economic development. But some relates to external resource piracy as in the unlicenced exploitation of fishing stocks or unsustainable forestry practices, and others to the effects of pollution or damage from the passage of tankers and cruise ships. Finally, there is a generalised risk of environmental deterioration from a number of sources including the transport and dumping of nuclear or other hazardous waste, the incidence of which has significantly increased in recent years, and the continuing effects of past nuclear testing in the South Pacific.

Threats to social cohesion

3.23 One of the strengths of many small countries is the relative degree of social homogeneity that prevails. Events or circumstances which undermine this constitute a threat. They can be transmitted via a number of channels. One which is very common is cultural penetration through the media. Small states depend on foreign broadcasting and are particularly open to foreign influences. This can undermine identity, tradition and custom leading to dissatisfaction and a sense of alienation, particularly among the young. Another is the backwash effect from the increased incidence of international travel. While there are considerable benefits and tangible rewards associated with international travel, the openness of small states provides fertile soil in which imported and different life-styles can flourish and which can be especially corrupting and destabilising when associated with drugs, leading to the weakening of social values which underpin the political system.

3.24 A number of small states are multi-ethnic, multi-religious and multi-cultural. While this can be a source of strength it can also be a source of weakness when divisions are highlighted or fostered for political advantage. This can come from outside the state and be the result of deliberate policy, or it can be more diffuse leading to an increased perception of those within the state as to their differences. When it occurs, the practice of accommodation between groups is put in jeopardy and political fears and tensions heightened, leading in some cases to armed action. While it is not the only example of such a threat the growth of religious fundamentalism in international politics has the potential to be particularly destabilising in such circumstances.

3.25 Unemployment levels in some small states are too high. While traditional extended family support systems and the habit of migration have ameliorated the immediate affects, changes internally and externally are making these more severe. Internally, the breakup of traditional systems and rapid urbanisation in small states have reduced the level and likelihood of support, whilst externally the flows of remittances back home are steadily reducing in volume and value over time. There is also a question over the future of emigration as an option as host states come under increasing pressure from their population to limit it. This is adding to the social costs of structural adjustment which some states have undergone. The unintended effect of many such programmes has been the growth of an 'informal' economic sector, thriving in the 'grey' area between legality and illegality, and living off services rendered in respect of money laundering, capital flight, exchange rate manipulation, corruption and unethical business and professional practice. More directly, crime has been encouraged through larceny, drug abuse and prostitution.

Threats and Vulnerability

3.26 While small states may be subjected to such threats it does not follow that any state will necessarily meet all of them, although it is our contention that the majority of small states will meet some, if not most of them, at some time or another. The principal determining factor will be the security environment in which they are located. While this has international and national elements the most important element for small states is the region. The setting of the various regions and their particular security threats are discussed in detail in Chapter 9.

3.27 It is also evident that threats will be perceived differently by small states, even within the same region, and that the impact of threats will vary considerably from state to state. The key element here is the individual circumstance of each state. This raises again the issue of vulnerability and underlines the proposition that what distinguishes small states from larger states is not the specificity of the threat they face but that should a threat become an actuality it is likely to be more difficult to resist and is likely to cause more harm than in other states.

4

The Economic Consequences of Smallness

4.1 Small economic size is widely believed to impose certain obstacles to economic development. While these were briefly surveyed in the *Vulnerability* report we amplify them here given the greater importance of the economic dimension for the future security and development of small states. The first section surveys some economic propositions relating to small states followed by a review of the latest evidence on the economic performance of small states.

Economic Consequences of Small Economic Size

4.2 There are considerable differences in average per capita incomes among small states and in their economic structure. These are given in Table 4.1 which contains data on the percentage distribution of GDP between three main economic sectors – agriculture (including fishing and forestry), industry (including manufacturing, mining, construction and utilities) and services for most countries earlier identified as small states. It shows that in the poorest states (Guyana and Lesotho excepted) agriculture is responsible for generating a large percentage of GDP and that most are comparatively unindustrialised. As per capita income rises, agriculture tends to diminish relatively as a source of income and industry accounts for a growing share of GDP. In some countries significant degrees of industrialisation have been achieved based on successful exploitation of mineral and fuel wealth and to a lesser extent on manufacturing. At the highest levels of income, services tend to be the most important sector with tourism and the provision of offshore financial services being particularly important. There are also some important regional differences. In the South Pacific the main sources of income are agriculture and services and the industrial sector is generally underdeveloped. In the Caribbean agriculture has declined and while industry remains significant in the economy, the service sector is growing rapidly. In several African small states industry (including manufacturing) has grown significantly in recent years.

4.3 Whatever their level of income or economic structure, all of them face obstacles to development on account of their small size. Two structural differences between small and large economies stand out. First, economic activities tend to be less diversified and more specialised than in large economies due to their narrower human and non-human

24

resource base and limited domestic market. While this constraint is observable in a range of activities it is most acutely felt in the inability of small states to sustain what may be termed 'advanced' branches of manufacturing industry, such as capital goods, metal-working and intermediate manufacturing sectors. These activities are characterised by economies of scale in production, product development and R&D and typically require a domestic market of a certain minimum size in order to become established. In their absence small states are typically more dependent on non-manufacturing (in the primary and tertiary sectors of the economy) as a source of output, employment and foreign exchange receipts or remain limited in their manufacturing capacity to basic 'low technology' manufacturing activities which are not affected by domestic market size.

4.4 Small states also suffer from diseconomies of scale in investment, transportation and the provision of government services. Generally, small countries suffer, to varying degrees, from higher unit costs of investment in the industrial sector, particularly in new technology and in capital intensive manufacturing, a disadvantage trade can only partly overcome. They also have higher per capita costs in establishing basic infrastructure because of higher unit costs. They also need more infra-structure per capita because of indivisibilities i.e. the provision of facilities that may not be fully used such as roads, airports, harbours and communication facilities. High per capita costs also arise in public administration where a minimum structure of government and level of services is necessary irrespective of size. At the same time, it follows that the smaller the country the more acute such diseconomies of scale are likely to be, with corresponding severe effects.

4.5 Second, small economies exhibit an exceptionally high degree of openness to external economic developments, in respect of trade, capital flows and technology. There are high levels of commodity export con-centration which limit possibilities for internal diversification. This makes for a high degree of sensitivity to, and dependence on, the international economic environment combined with a limited capacity to stabilise the domestic economy in the face of external shocks. In short, small states suffer a greatly reduced degree of national economic sovereignty and limited capacity to control domestic economic variables so as to affect their own economic destiny.

4.6 In practice, it is this second structural characteristic of openness which has come to dominate the discussion on small state economic disadvantage. It emphasises the vulnerability of small states and there-fore requires further consideration. At the same time, openness can provide opportunities and benefits for small states. This is noted on page 27 as well as in the discussion on globalisation.

Table 4.1 Small States*: Per Capita GNP and Distribution of GDP, 1995
(countries ranked by per capita GNP)

	Per Capita GNP US$	Sectoral Distribution of GDP (%)		
		Agriculture	Industry	Services
Guinea-Bissau	250	47	18	35
The Gambia	320	28	15	58
Sao Tome e Principe	350	21	26	53
Equatorial Guinea	380	50	33	17
Comoros	470	39	13	48
Guyana	590	39	23	38
Lesotho	770	10	56	34
Djibouti	780 (93)	3	21	76
Suriname	880	26	26	48
Solomon Islands	910	44	3	53
Kiribati	920	24	9	67
Cape Verde	960	7	14	79
Maldives	990	22	17	61
Tuvalu	1,050 (94)	n/a	n/a	n/a
Samoa	1,120	40	20	40
Papua New Guinea	1,160	26	42	32
Swaziland	1,170	12	39	50
Vanuatu	1,200	20	14	66
Jamaica	1,510	8	41	51
Tonga	1,630	38	19	43
Namibia	2,000	11	26	63
St Vincent and the Grenadines	2,280	10	19	71
Fiji	2,440	21	18	61
Belize	2,630	20	27	53
Grenada	2,980	11	19	70
Dominica	2,990	21	22	57
Botswana	3,020	6	47	47
St Lucia	3,370	11	14	75
Mauritius	3,380	9	32	59
Trinidad and Tobago	3,770	2	43	55
Gabon	3,980	8	53	39
St Kitts and Nevis	5,170	6	25	69
Barbados	6,560	5	16	79
Seychelles	6,620	4	15	81
Antigua and Barbuda	7,330	4	19	77
Bahrain	7,840	1	42	57
Malta	7,970 (93)	3	35	62
Nauru	8,070 (93)	n/a	n/a	n/a
Cyprus	10,380	6	25	69
The Bahamas	11,940	2	14	83
Brunei Darussalam	14,240 (94)	3	52	45

*Reliable data for Micronesia, Marshall Islands and Palau listed in table 2.1 are not available; Commonwealth countries are shown in **bold**.

Source: World Bank data base and Commonwealth Secretariat, Small States: Economic Review and Basic Statistics, 1997.

Trade openness

4.7 Trade openness is seen in an economy in which many of the goods produced are exported, many of the goods sold imported, and in which services, some of which such as tourism and offshore banking are primarily directed at foreigners, are very important. High trade openness increases a country's vulnerability to external shocks. Such shocks on the export side, whether of demand and/or supply, can affect both the price and/or quantity of exports and cause considerable short-term instability in export earnings. This, in turn, can transmit into instability in final demand – in the absence of adequate stabilising measures – an effect which will be greater the more open the economy. Instability in domestic demand may have adverse consequences, due to enhanced uncertainty, on the level of investment and, hence, on the long-term growth rate of the economy. Meanwhile, prolonged depression in relative primary product prices, such as occurred during the 1980s can, through the loss of dynamism imparted to the growth of final demand and the imposition of constraints on the real capacity to import, impart strong stagnationist tendencies to the medium-term growth rate.

4.8 On the import side, external shocks consist principally of price changes which in a very open economy have the capacity to impart strong inflationary or deflationary impulses to the domestic price level. Not all small states are highly 'open' on the export side. Some, especially a number of small South Pacific island economies, have such a weak resource base and a consequent dearth of international competitive exports that their export: GDP ratios are quite low. High trade openness for them expresses itself in a high ratio of imports: GDP – and, given the weaknesses on the export side, the resulting substantial external trade imbalance can only be sustained by resort to transfers from abroad (including intergovernmental transfers and workers' remittances).

4.9 At the same time it is important to recognise that trade openness can be a source of strength as well as weakness: a source of vitality as well as vulnerability. A country which derives a large proportion of final demand from exports has potential international dynamism so long as the country's exports are located in dynamic, rapidly-expanding branches of world trade. Rapid growth of export earnings can result in rapid increases in efficiency and product quality and rapid increases in the capacity to import, thereby releasing the restriction posed by the foreign exchange constraint on growth.

Commodity export concentration

4.10 In Commonwealth small states exports account for well over 50% of GDP in the majority of countries. A feature of export patterns is a high degree of specialisation in a narrow range of products in order to secure economies of scale in production, marketing, transportation and distribution. Such specialisation increases a country's exposure to export price and quantity risk in the short-term, giving rise to earnings instability. Also in the medium and long-term, a country may find its resources excessively committed to slowly growing segments of world trade. Where a high degree of commodity concentration is linked to a dominant (i.e. price-setting) position in world trade, price and quantity movements may be off-set. However, most small states, even where their commodity exports are highly concentrated, are unlikely to be price-setters.

4.11 Export diversification generally serves to reduce the price and quantity risks due to concentration. In practice, many small states have experienced quite considerable diversification of their export earnings in recent years. Their commodity exports have been diversified via the growth of manufactured exports as well as non-traditional primary products. Furthermore, in many small states, exports of goods now constitute barely a majority of their total exports due to the rapid growth of 'invisible' earnings from tourism, offshore banking and other financial services and workers' remittances.

Dependence on foreign resource flows

4.12 Various studies have shown that small countries experience a larger (net) transfer of foreign resources (as measured by the deficit on trade in goods and non-factor services) relative to GNP than larger countries. They also enjoy relatively greater resort to public concessional finance which assists in holding down their debt-servicing burdens. However, small countries are more constrained in their access to the world's fast-growing sources of private finance. Small countries' high degree of 'openness' on the capital account, whilst to some degree beneficial in enabling them to absorb foreign resources, makes them vulnerable to capital flow instability.

Limited capacity to manage the economic environment

4.13 Because of their openness on both trade and capital accounts small countries are both vulnerable to economic shocks originating from abroad and find it difficult to offset them through national macroeconomic management. In a situation where imports satisfy such a large share of domestic spending, small countries have little control over the domestic price level. Sudden dramatic changes in prices for imports or exports will be quickly transmitted to domestic activity levels causing considerable fluctuations in income unless some form of stabilisation is available to cushion their effect. Similarly, withdrawal of official finance can, through cuts in the development budget and even current spending, impart major depressive effects on the level of activity.

4.14 Insulation from such external shocks can, in principle, be achieved by a flexible exchange rate. But, in a highly open economy, large exchange rate fluctuations produce big internal price and cost disturbances. Small countries, therefore, tend to peg their exchange rates to the currencies of their main trading partners and some even adopt their currency. While there can be economic gains from such a strategy there is also clearly loss of policy autonomy with the added risk that the small state exposes itself to exchange rate fluctuations stemming from fluctuations in the value of the dominant currency.

4.15 In countries with a fixed exchange rate and without capital controls, there is little scope for monetary policy to affect prices and quantities in the non-traded sector of the economy. Thus, the impact of an expansionary monetary policy, through lowering interest rates, may be offset by induced capital outflow (and lower remittances) and have little impact on levels of economic activity. Similarly, a contractionary monetary policy may be offset by capital inflow. Where small countries adopt currency boards or allow a foreign currency to circulate as the domestic medium, they shed their last vestiges of monetary autonomy.

High international transport costs

4.16 The majority of small developing economies are island states and three of them in Southern Africa are landlocked. Because of the relatively small volumes of cargo carried, as well as the remoteness of island economies and the difficult terrain of landlocked economies, small countries suffer high international transport costs per unit value of goods transported. This has the effect of increasing domestic costs of consumption and production and the cif (cost-insurance-freight) delivery price of exports relative to competitors. Small states on average pay 10% as freight costs against the global average of 4.5% and 8.3% for all developing countries. This represents a further impediment to successful economic development which small island states, in particular, are unable to effectively counter given their limited bargaining power with the shipping lines and the prohibitive costs of establishing their own merchant marines.

The Recent Economic Performance of Small States

4.17 In spite of these constraints, the empirical evidence shows that the economic performance of small developing countries since 1980 has been no worse than that of larger countries – indeed, if anything, slightly superior. This suggests either that the obstacles mentioned earlier are not so serious or that small developing states found ways of overcoming or compensating for them. Another possibility is that large countries were affected by adverse developments since 1980 not shared to the same degree by small countries. Indeed, one obvious factor stands out: namely, the developing country debt crisis, as a result of which for many countries the 1980s were a 'lost decade' in terms of economic progress and, for others, even worse, a period of considerable regression. Small countries, failing to gain access to private bank credits in the 1970s, escaped the worst effects of the crisis and painful adjustment in the 1980s.

4.18 At the same time, empirical evidence also suggests that per capita GDP growth is subject to wider fluctuations in small developing states relative to large states, although there is clearly a very considerable degree of variation in fluctuations between countries which is not accounted for by population size. Uganda, a medium sized country, exhibits very high fluctuations as do large countries such as China and Bangladesh. These cases suggest that important sources of economic instability, such as political upheaval, policy switches and natural disasters cannot be ignored. The impact of the latter on SIDS is a matter of record.

4.19 Finally, note must be taken of the many and varied sources of economic growth in small states. Traditional primary products exports are still proportionately large in many countries' export receipts and though of diminishing importance have served as significant sources of employment in the agricultural sector. Remittances remain important for some states and logging and mineral extraction continue to be a source of economic growth, although of late there has been considerable concern expressed about the sustainability of such activity. Some countries recorded manufacture export-oriented growth, particularly in clothing and textiles. Others saw particularly rapid growth in tourism and in offshore banking, insurance and other services. All this suggests that while smallness does limit the capacity to transform such economies it is not an insuperable obstacle to diversification and development. Similarly, openness can be a source of advantage as well as vulnerability.

5

The Economic Dimension: Analysis

5.1 In the past decade the world economy has been transformed by dynamic changes. With the ending of the Cold War, the ideological debate about alternative approaches to economic development has ended with a consensus emerging on the relevance and importance of market forces as determinants of economic performance. The globalisation of production and the liberalisation of trade have increased the challenges facing developing countries. Advances in technology and the increased mobility of capital have improved the prospects for productivity gains and wealth creation. In some cases, new regional arrangements have opened new opportunities in trade and related economic policy areas. Increased interdependence and insistent competitive pressures have become the distinguishing features of the contemporary global economy, determining the position of countries within it and shaping their possibilities for economic development.

5.2 The concern of many small developing states is that they will be disadvantaged in the emerging global economic order and that some will be further marginalised in world trade, investment, commodities and capital markets. This is a real fear every bit as worrying as the threat of intervention in the Cold War. The discussion of security in Chapter 3 drew attention to threats which could significantly narrow the range of policy options available to the state or to private non-governmental entities within the state. Some countries risk such an outcome unless early positive action is taken by them to improve their competitiveness through domestic policy reform and to enhance their prospects for growth through integration into the global economy.

5.3 The focus of this chapter and the following one is on the adjustments small states will need to make to survive globalisation and its related process of regionalisation. They examine the impact globalisation has had upon them and set out the domestic reforms small states will need to implement nationally, as well as the initiatives they will need to take regionally, to maximise opportunities and minimise constraints.

The Effects of Globalisation

5.4 The importance of openness in promoting economic development is one of the more insistent themes that has emerged from an understanding of the processes of globalisation. Many analysts, led by the World Bank, have argued that countries which have integrated into the world economy are better off: trade has grown, flows of private capital have increased, and as a consequence rates of economic growth have risen. Developing countries which have embarked on policy reforms to open their economies to the domestic and international market have had an advantage over those that have not.

5.5 Others, however, argue that globalisation has only benefited a handful of larger countries in East Asia, Latin America and Eastern Europe, and that there are many negative aspects. They claim that countries have lost policy autonomy; domination of transnational corporations has increased; and large scale capital movements, particularly those of a speculative nature, have introduced greater volatility, and thereby contributed to greater instability, in financial markets.

5.6 Such observations, while often merited on both sides, do not address the issue from the point of view of the small state. The handicaps of size and the associated consequences pose additional burdens and challenges which are rarely acknowledged. The World Bank routinely excludes small countries with a population size of less than one million from many of its studies. Its recent report *Global Economic Prospects* (1996), which presents data on the pace of global integration for 93 countries, provides information on only four small countries (Jamaica, Trinidad and Tobago, Botswana and Mauritius). Of these, the World Bank categorises only Mauritius as a successful integrator. Furthermore, the analysis of country situations and characteristics excludes any reference to size as a factor in the ability to integrate.

5.7 Nevertheless, it would appear that a number of other small states – Barbados, Botswana, Cyprus, The Gambia, Guyana, Jamaica, Malta and Trinidad and Tobago – have been successful in integrating into the world economy and that globalisation has made a positive contribution to their economic performance. They have not only expanded their production and export base through diversification, but have experienced expanded capital flows. Their overall growth rates have, on average, improved and are comparable to the favourable rates enjoyed by larger countries. These countries have had favourable external markets largely because of preferential entry to major markets for their goods and/or because of proximity to near by markets for goods and services. Policy reforms have also played a significant role in improving the overall performance.

5.8 However, it can also be argued that the pace of reforms in several of these countries was accelerated precisely because they enjoyed the initial advantages linked with location, assured markets for traditional products, and access to capital, often grant aid, which permitted the implementation of reforms. A large number of small states, especially in Africa and the South Pacific did not have comparable advantages and have found it next to impossible to move very far down the path of integration into the world economy. Because of their size and the structure of their economies, which have a narrow production base, fragile fiscal systems, a high degree of export concentration, limited opportunities for diversification and privatisation of state-owned enterprises, and a relatively undeveloped private sector, the scope for reforms has been limited. These small states in Africa and the South Pacific regions, have been caught in a vicious cycle and have become increasingly marginalised and face threats to living standards in the future.

5.9 It is difficult to state conclusively the role that size has played in this situation as larger countries with similar characteristics have also not performed well and have failed to integrate into the world economy. There is, however, a distinct policy dimension to those that have succeeded in doing so. The impetus for globalisation has come largely from domestic policy reforms mounted by governments, in part driven by the need to undertake structural adjustments. The Bretton Woods organisations have led the way in espousing the need for reforms. These include trade liberalisation through a lowering of tariffs and the removal of non-tariff barriers, including the lifting of quantitative restrictions; exchange rate adjustments with the goal of improving the competitiveness of exports and the attainment of external equilibrium; and fiscal reforms both on the revenue and expenditure side of public finances. Tax reforms have largely focused on introducing greater competitiveness, the elimination of disincentives to investment and enhancement of entrepreneurial activity. Revenue structures have been changed to emphasise taxes on consumption. On the expenditure side cost cutting, removal of subsidies and privatisation of state-owned enterprises have been favoured instruments to attain the overall goal of a reduction of public sector deficits. Taken together, these policies have contributed to the emergence of a greater market-oriented regime while at the same time setting in place greater macroeconomic stability. They have led to greater investment, expanded trade and inward flows of foreign private capital, and generally have helped create a more open economy.

5.10 The following sections examine the trade, financial, technological and communication patterns that impact on small countries, and evaluate the extent to which they have been capable of embarking upon domestic policy reforms. Given the importance attached to the private sector in taking advantage of opportunities presented by such reform the final section examines its role.

Trade

5.11 Most Commonwealth small states can be grouped into four major categories in terms of their export orientation: agriculture and fisheries; petroleum and minerals; tourism and services; and a group that has a mixture of one or more of the above with manufactures as a new element in the production base. As noted earlier, the contribution of exports of goods and services to GDP is high in most of them, with exports accounting for well over 50% of total GDP in the majority of these countries.

5.12 A feature of export patterns is the narrow range of products. Bananas are a major commodity in the exports of several Caribbean countries, accounting for almost 70% in the case of Dominica, 60% in the case of St Lucia, and 42% in the case of St Vincent and the Grenadines. Production is largely by small operators with low acreage, and export is directed to the European Union (EU) with low or non-existent tariffs. Sugar is another mainstay of several Caribbean, Indian Ocean and South Pacific island countries; it accounts for more than 25% of merchandise export earnings for Belize, Fiji, Guyana and Mauritius.

5.13 Textiles and garments are significant export commodities in several Caribbean countries, including Barbados, Belize, Jamaica, St Lucia and Trinidad and Tobago. Textile exports are of importance to Cyprus, Fiji, Mauritius, Tonga and Vanuatu. The exports are destined to the major markets in close proximity, North America in the case of the Caribbean, the European Union (EU) for the Mediterranean countries and Australia-New Zealand for the South Pacific states. Several of the South Pacific and Indian Ocean countries – Maldives, Papua New Guinea, Seychelles and Solomon Islands – have developed their fishery resources and the industry makes a significant contribution to their exports. Petroleum product exports account for almost two-thirds of the exports of Trinidad and Tobago and even more for Brunei. Minerals are a significant item of export in the case of Guyana and Papua New Guinea. Several countries, particularly in the South Pacific, have seen wood and timber-based products emerge as significant export commodities. This is also true in the cases of Belize and Guyana. Diversified manufactures, largely consisting of electronics, are exported from a handful of countries – Barbados, Malta and Mauritius.

5.14 The growth of service exports has largely been in the form of tourism, and offshore banking and financial services. Service exports have become a significant source of income for small island states in the Caribbean and the South Pacific. Cyprus, Maldives, Mauritius and Seychelles have also expanded their tourism industries. As a source of export earnings, tourism now contributes more than the export of primary commodities in several South Pacific states. In the case of Vanuatu, as much as a quarter of the GDP could be attributed to tourism. Kiribati, Solomon Islands and Tonga also have substantial earnings from tourism – between 4% and 7% of GDP. In the Caribbean earnings from tourism amounted to US$ 11.7 billion in 1994.

5.15 Information processing has emerged as a new service sector activity but has not expanded beyond a small number of Caribbean countries to other regions. Barbados, Grenada, Jamaica, St Lucia and Trinidad and Tobago are countries that have an export-based information processing industry. However, the overall contribution of the industry in each of the economies is relatively small. Over the past two decades the Caribbean region has become a leading provider of offshore banking and financial services, taking advantage of the demand for diversified offshore services. In global terms, 74% of the total number of offshore companies registered in island jurisdictions are in the Caribbean – The Bahamas, Cayman Islands and the Netherlands Antilles. Modest developments have also taken place in other regions. In the South Pacific some small states have established offshore banking and related services. In Vanuatu 10% of the GDP is estimated to arise from the exports of such services. Malta and Cyprus also have such facilities with over 22,000 offshore trading entities registered in Cyprus alone.

5.16 Trade by destination has continued to follow traditional patterns and been determined by the preferences accorded by the major trading partners in respect of particular commodity groups. Geographic proximity has also been a factor. The Caribbean states export a significant volume of their output to North America and the EU. Bananas and sugar enjoy preferential access under the Lomé regime established by the EU. The Multi-Fibre Arrangement (MFA) regime, along with the US sponsored Caribbean Basin Initiative (CBI) and Canadian CARIBCAN arrangements have provided several countries with preferential entry for textiles to many markets. In the case of the South Pacific Island States, the South Pacific Regional Trade and Economic Co-operation Agreement (SPARTECA) sponsored by Australia and New Zealand has provided preferential treatment to these countries. The Generalised System of Preferences (GSP) has played a role too in providing access in other developed industrial country markets, especially Japan. Some South Pacific states have also benefited under Lomé. In brief, not only has trade flowed to markets where preferences exist, but its growth has been determined by the nature of the preferences extended. While this does more to preserve the past than to promote the future, it must be acknowledged that for many small states commodity exports are the bedrock of the economy and an indispensable base for successful diversification. Proposals to phase out preferences are therefore alarming for many small states without significant compensatory measures being agreed.

Financial markets and capital flows

5.17 It has been claimed that small countries generally have limited access to capital, both from private markets and from multilateral financial institutions such as the World Bank. There is some truth to this contention. In general, private capital markets tend to favour larger countries on creditworthiness grounds and on past lender–borrower relationships. Small countries have no significant track record and are at a disadvantage. Foreign direct investment (FDI) tends to gravitate to countries with a strong track record of political stability, a hospitable environment for FDI, good infrastructure, and an adequate pool of skilled labour. While many of these conditions can be found in some small countries, they are counterbalanced by the size and viability issue. The attractiveness of large markets and readily available domestic joint venture partners are other factors that place large countries at an advantage. Multilateral lending institutions are constrained by portfolio considerations and tend to limit their exposure in small countries. But more critically, the many small countries with relatively high per capita GNP levels, for instance in the Caribbean, are excluded from receiving the International Development Association (IDA) credits because of their income levels. Thus, these states are unable to tap both the private markets and the multilateral sources of capital on concessional terms. They are excessively dependent on bilateral grants for their external capital requirements. Grant aid, in general, is subject to the vagaries of budgetary conditions in the donor countries, thus increasing uncertainties for the recipients. Furthermore, the aid policies of the bilateral donors favour the poorest countries, so designated on the basis of GNP per capita estimates.

5.18 A review of the trends in the inflow of external capital since the late 1970s indicates that all developing countries recorded sizeable inflows. The small states, in the aggregate, shared in these inflows in the late 1970s and the early 1980s and were largely able to cushion the impact of the oil crisis. However, slow adjustment and the general global declines in capital flows in the late 1980s affected small states more severely. In the Caribbean, net external capital inflows declined sharply from US\$ 420 million in 1982 to US\$ 250 million in 1990. In terms of net transfers, these turned negative in 1990 and continue to remain negative. However, in comparative terms, small states, while badly affected, may have fared no worse than larger countries that were forced into adjustment. Indeed, in one sense they are at an advantage because of the low level of debt and debt service. However, the process of adjustment for several small states has been drawn out and painful. In the absence of a strong macroeconomic environment and with a relatively weak economic base, small countries continue to be more vulnerable to uncertainties about the future flows of external capital flows on a sustained basis.

5.19 The growth in net FDI flows to developing countries, from a level of US$ 24.0 billion in 1990 to US$ 80.1 billion in 1994, may well bypass most small states. Of the total net flow in 1994, only US$ 0.9 billion or a little over 1% went to small countries. What is more significant is that the share of the small countries was a little over 2.6% at US$ 0.62 billion in 1990. Very small states start out with low bargaining power with respect to major external investors. Many transnational corporations have incomes larger than the GNP of these small states. The danger of dependency is enhanced, and the small state may not have the opportunity to benefit from technological innovation because of low participation by local suppliers.

5.20 Global declines in the flow of concessional assistance, both multi-lateral and bilateral, particularly grant-type assistance, will in the short-term impose additional challenges for many small states. Grants, which have been the mainstay of resource flows, will decline further. In the first place, the pool of concessional resources will shrink as donors curtail contributions to the World Bank's IDA and other concessional funds managed by regional banks. Concurrently, bilateral aid budgets are being curtailed in part driven by domestic budgetary austerity. Bilateral donors have in recent years deliberately introduced policies that tend to direct their aid allocations to the poorest countries where poverty levels are high and to those 'countries in transition' to which high political priorities apply. Taking these various trends into account, the many small states which are also middle income developing states are likely to face reductions in the levels of concessional assistance.

5.21 While this is clearly a matter of concern in the long term, the impact in the short and medium term is likely to be blunted by the difficulties encountered in many small states in preparing project dossiers and accessing concessional assistance. The immediate problem in many of them is less the availability of concessional finance than technical shortages and a lack of initial start-up funds. In so far as these are important constraints on development they require urgent attention, both in terms of demands made by donors to small states in terms of preparing and servicing projects and programmes, and by small states in developing human capacity.

5.22 Small states have had limited access to multilateral loans, in part because of creditworthiness concerns dictated by the desire of the IFIs to maintain overall portfolio profiles that minimise risks. Additionally, some high income small states have been precluded from borrowing from IFI resources because of the policy of graduating countries above a given per capita income level. In the near term, additional countries such as Antigua and Barbuda, St Kitts and Nevis and the Seychelles, are likely to be graduated. In a sense, success in economic performance is likely to penalise these high income countries through exclusion from lending by the IFIs. Such countries, once cut loose by the IFIs, face the challenge of borrowing in capital markets. Small states are handicapped in a number of significant ways. In the eyes of the market lenders, they are judged less creditworthy and face greater difficulties in borrowing, or at the very least are only able to borrow on terms which are unfavourable. Not only are they required to pay interest charges above average market terms, but they also cannot in all circumstances obtain longer maturities.

5.23 Whereas the larger developing countries, which have over the years developed their domestic capital markets, have been able to attract portfolio funds, most small states have been unable to do so. Developing capital markets in small states is a formidable proposition. These states have a limited capacity to promote and operate efficient stock exchanges as there is likely to be only a handful of enterprises that could be floated. While larger countries have strengthened their capital markets through privatisation, the scope for this is far more limited and cannot be a factor in the development of a functioning capital market which would attract external portfolio resources. Under these circumstances, most small states are unlikely to benefit from the global growth in portfolio flows.

5.24 The best prospect for external finance for many small states is represented by tapping into flows of FDI. Although several small states have benefited from the flows of FDI which have contributed to their diversification effort, leading in turn to export growth and income growth, these rewards have flowed in part from several factors. They include: their proximity to large markets and/or well developed transport links; the natural resource base in the form of climatic and geographic advantages that are conducive to the development of tourism; socio-economic political stability; the presence of a human resource base for use in the development of services e.g. tourism, banking and offshore financial services; and a reasonably well developed infrastructure, particularly in telecommunications. Additionally, a hospitable investment climate reflected by openness to trade and investment underpinned by both domestic policies – fiscal, regulatory frameworks – and external policies that commit the country to international agreements on Trade Related Investment Measures (TRIMs) and Trade Related Intellectual

Property Rights (TRIPs) are significant. A competitive environment in terms of labour costs is important, as are investment incentives.

5.25 The challenge for small states is therefore how to tap into the global FDI market. However, this will require the institution of a whole range of policies that impact on the investment environment. While policies do matter and will continue to be a determining factor, there is no absolute guarantee that small states will be successful in a highly competitive environment.

New communications technologies and their impact

5.26 The integration of the world economy and the trend towards globalisation has in part been facilitated by technological advances that have improved communications and information flows. Telecommunications now form an indispensable part of the infrastructure of a modern economy and provide the means to both transmit and process information. Information is fast emerging as an important input into the production process, be it in trading commodities, underpinning a range of financial services, or in the manufacturing process. For small states, particularly those that are remote from the major markets and commercial and financial centres, the communications revolution has created the possibility of reducing traditional barriers and opened up new opportunities. For many small island states, remoteness, smallness and isolation can be overcome and the development of modern telecommunication capacities could become the engine for growth, development and diversification of the economic base.

5.27 The role that telecommunications can play in small states in the various facets of development merits close attention. Communication links between somewhat isolated communities within an archipelago, or even on a single island, are often underdeveloped. Putting in place facilities that permit the exchange and transmission of information can bring about greater cohesiveness and a sense of unity that contributes to a lessening of the threat to security. In the economic context, the ability to transmit information rapidly permits the authorities to provide early warning of approaching cyclones and hurricanes. The facilities in place can also permit speedier dissemination of other relevant information e.g. changes in external prices. In the political and administrative context, they can provide greater efficiency and more effective management of resources and make a contribution to good governance which reduces the security risk while enhancing the prospects for sustainable development.

5.28 The role of telecommunications in promoting tourism can be significant. The industry is highly dependent on contacts with agents and travel services abroad. Telecommunications are also important to visitors who need to be in contact with the outside world. Good external communications are also critical in the context of the offshore banking and financial services industries. The globalisation of capital markets has been made possible by the rapid development of telecommunication and information links. Thus small states that are entering the field will need to be linked into global networks. The availability of efficient information and communication links has the psychological benefits of reducing the sense of isolation as small states begin to feel that they are a part of a global village. For island and archipelagic states, aerial surveillance of EEZs against foreign illegal fishing, using modern communications, is important.

5.29 Many small states have made commendable progress in acquiring telecommunication capacities. The Caribbean has an average of 167 telephone lines per 100 inhabitants and the South Pacific small states 24.6. The Indian Ocean small island states of Mauritius and Seychelles have higher densities than South Africa. The Caribbean states have taken advantage of their telecommunication infrastructure to develop information processing for North American enterprises. The Barbados authorities have identified informatics as one of the areas with great potential for development.

5.30 Estimates prepared by the International Telecommunications Union indicate that small island states invested almost half a billion dollars in 1994 in developing their telecommunication facilities. Revenue earned amounted to almost US$2 billion and accounted for almost 2% of the GDP of these states, and was growing rapidly. The potential exists for further growth and development, but will require the adoption of policies that aim to maximise the contribution of the sector. Apart from creating the appropriate macroeconomic policies and the promotion of new investment, governments will need to address issues of competition amongst providers to ensure that over-capacity is not created. Some regulation of the industry would be necessary to ensure that consumer interests are safeguarded. Given that many small states lie in climatic zones subjected to hurricanes and cyclones, future investment in lines should be in the form of underground facilities in order to protect the investment. Most small states have shortages of skilled telecommunication workers. In the overall programme for human resource development, it would be necessary to assign high priority to the training of workers for employment in this sector.

The role of the private sector

5.31 The private sector in most small states is made up of small and medium sized enterprises. The size of the domestic market is a constraining factor in the growth of enterprises. In addition, in the past public ownership of many businesses has crowded out private enterprise that would have otherwise emerged. The governments of many small states have tended to emphasise the role of public sector-led development. Centrally managed responses to issues of external resource mobilisation and emphasis on social equity issues are other factors that have tended to downplay the role of the private sector. Tax regimes, structured around trade taxes and surcharges, and the dominant role of state-owned marketing boards in both exporting and importing goods, have inhibited the emergence of private businesses. In some instances these boards have enjoyed monopoly rights, thus precluding entry into areas which otherwise would have been occupied by private investors. Many governments of small states play a major role in reviewing and approving investment decisions. While some of these practices are legitimate functions and are in the public interest, poor administrative practices increase the cost of doing business and act as a deterrent to business expansion. The absence of transparency in decision-making processes is an additional barrier. The inherent bias of policies contributes to making some small states less attractive to investors. Foreign investors often are unable to find local joint venture partners.

5.32 In recent years, some progress has been made in changing the business climate. The governments of many small states have begun liberalising the economy. A range of activities are being privatised and efforts are being made to harness the energies of the private sector to become the main engine of growth, through investment and job creation. Changes in the tax and regulatory regimes are having the desired impact in several small states. However, the pace of change is uneven. Some Caribbean and Mediterranean states, along with Mauritius, are moving ahead with policy reforms and have been rewarded with an acceleration in growth. Progress in other regions is slow and their economic performance continues to be sluggish. The role of the Chambers of Commerce and the Manufacturers' Association can be critical in developing positions on specific issues at annual conferences for the exchange of ideas. There needs to be an on-going effort drawing on the experience of existing private sector institutional agencies.

Trends in Regionalisation

5.33 The growth of regionalisation is widely interpreted as a response to globalisation. At its heart is a state-driven project to harness the benefits and minimise the costs of globalisation. Regionalisation is therefore a process feeding the globalisation process, not contradictory to it. It is best seen in the espousal of 'open regionalism' by the three major blocs of the EU, NAFTA and APEC; and the impetus to a 'new regionalism' in the developing world. 'Open regionalism' is based on the principles of free-market capitalism. It has two fundamental characteristics: (1) within a given geographical region obstacles to trade are steadily reduced as at the same time obligations to the WTO are observed i.e. external tariff barriers to the rest of the world are not increased; (2) new opportunities in technology, investment and financial liberalisation are encouraged, regionally and globally, with the goal of improving national, regional and international competitiveness. 'Open regionalism' is both inward and outward looking, seeing the region as an arena in which the agenda of liberalisation can be advanced more speedily and to the benefit of the participating countries than can be done globally. 'New regionalism' in the developing world is similarly imbued with liberal principles. It is also outward looking and it is this feature which distinguishes it from previous experiences of regional integration which were more inward looking and dirigiste in their policies and objectives.

5.34 The promotion of 'open regionalism' and 'new regionalism', alongside globalisation, is of particular importance to many small states. Most of them have preferential trade arrangements with neighbouring countries and with extra-regional groupings which are being eroded and revised in the wake of globalisation. The most important extra-regional grouping, in the sense that it has trade and aid programmes of direct interest to nearly all the Commonwealth small states, is the EU. Cyprus and Malta have association agreements with the EU and both have applied for entry, although Malta has for the moment decided not to proceed. The others, with the exception of the Brunei, Maldives and Nauru, are party to the Lomé Convention which is a comprehensive aid and trade agreement between the 15 members of the EU and 70 countries in Africa, the Caribbean and the Pacific (ACP).

5.35 Other arrangements are more region specific, but what is clear in all of them is that adjustments are having to be made and that old relationships are being revised as well as new organisations being created. In this new world there is a great deal of uncertainty as to whether small states will be able to find a place and voice in new regional arrangements. There is also a question as to whether they will be able to benefit as much as larger states from the opportunities provided. The following section reviews the major regional challenges facing small states.

The Lomé Convention

5.36 The Lomé Convention was first signed in 1975 and it has been periodically re-negotiated since to add new co-operation instruments and to set new priorities in development assistance. The present Convention ends in the year 2000. There is considerable uncertainty about the shape and scope of any future agreement in view of the changes in the world trade regime brought about by the Uruguay Round agreements and the decision of the EU to redefine its external relations to give greater prominence to the common foreign and security goals of member states. The EU is also reviewing its development co-operation policy, including the importance of its preferential trade regimes and the value of its programmes of technical and financial assistance.

5.37 Some of the changes the EU may wish to see in any new agreement with the ACP, or specific regions within it, have been proposed in a Green Paper released by the European Commission in November 1996. Several of the ideas in the Green Paper have already been incorporated in the Lomé Convention. These include a greater emphasis on structured political dialogue, stricter conditionality on aid, increased emphasis on the private sector and other non-governmental organisations (NGOs) in delivering development, and new requirements for developing countries to respect human rights, good governance and the rule of law. Other ideas are relatively new and include a phased end to non-reciprocal trade preferences, emphasis on improving the competitiveness of developing countries to enable them to fully engage with the global economy, a focus on poverty reduction in the delivery of aid programmes, and a greater awareness of differentiation among the ACP in respect of the need for trading preference, the reliance on aid and geographic location. This last element has raised the possibility of region specific agreements which would be part of a new Convention or be separately concluded with the Caribbean, the South Pacific and the African countries, thereby spelling the end of the ACP as a group and of the Convention as it has developed to date.

5.38 The response of the ACP to many of these proposals is likely to be negative. They have already indicated a preference to stay together and to preserve as many benefits from the present Convention as possible. In respect of the Commonwealth small states this means maintaining the protocols in sugar, bananas and beef. There is also a desire to maintain preferential access to the EU market and the distinctive development assistance programme administered by the European Commission. Other areas of common interest include the special programmes for island developing countries, land-locked countries and the least developed countries. Finally, the institutional arrangements in the Convention provide an unparalleled opportunity for Commonwealth small states to engage in dialogue and develop common positions with nine other small developing states who are not members of the Commonwealth but are party to the Lomé Convention.

The Caribbean

5.39 The major regional organisation is the Caribbean Community (CARICOM) which was created in 1973. It includes all the Commonwealth Caribbean small states plus Montserrat and Suriname. Recently Haiti has been accepted for membership. It established a common market for the purposes of trade and economic co-operation, defined various functional areas for co-operation, and provided for the co-ordination of foreign policies among member states. The Common Market has survived but it has not proved to be a dynamic instrument for development and has attracted much criticism on this account. Major proposals for change in the early 1990s, as well as fears of marginalisation from the global economy, have recently led to renewed impetus to achieve a single market and economy. While this is now set for 1999 the question of the further development of CARICOM depends on a number of factors including political will and external developments such as the proposed Free Trade Area of the Americas (FTAA). There is also the special position of the smaller Eastern Caribbean countries, grouped in the sub-regional Organisation of Eastern Caribbean States (OECS), to consider. Their interests regarding trading arrangements are likely to be different from the larger Caribbean countries.

5.40 A new regional organisation, the Association of Caribbean States (ACS), was established in July 1994. It arose from a proposal for a basin-wide regional organisation to take account of rapid changes in the Americas which were creating areas of common interest between all the Caribbean states (including non-independent territories) and states on the littoral. The present membership of 25 includes all the independent Caribbean states plus those in Central America and the Group of Three (Colombia, Mexico and Venezuela). The ACS is defined as 'an organisation for consultation, co-operation and concerted action'. It has identified some areas for action, including trade liberalisation, tourism and transport, but it has yet to project a distinctive presence in the region. There are many reasons for this including historically based and contemporary obstacles to closer co-operation between CARICOM and Latin American countries. However, what is clear is that the ACS is expected to play a role complementary to that of CARICOM, not to be an alternative or substitute for it. In this sense its function is to project a larger presence for the Caribbean than they might otherwise be able to achieve.

5.41 The small states in the Caribbean are party to the Lomé Convention. This has provided significant trade advantages to the Caribbean as well as being a source of financial and technical assistance. The Caribbean, along with other ACP states, is currently engaged in a debate on what future arrangements will govern its relations with the EU after 2000. The Caribbean position is to retain as many of the advantages from the present Convention as possible, particularly in respect of trade and the protocols for sugar and bananas. The EU is more open as to future arrangements. It is not possible at present to determine the likely course or outcome of negotiations. It is expected, however, that the EU will continue to maintain an interest in the region. The question is how broadly this will be cast. Among the options trailed for future arrangements is a wider regional agreement to include the states of Central America. Another is a free trade area. Whatever transpires it is likely that the Caribbean will find that any new arrangement is not as beneficial in trade or in aid.

5.42 'Open regionalism' is most unsettling for the Caribbean in its relationship with the US. The US has initiated a regionalist project in the Americas built around the construction of a hemispheric free trade alliance. To date the most important elements have been the establishment of the NAFTA and the proposal to create a FTAA by 2005. The potential for the Caribbean to be disadvantaged by these developments is very high. To begin with the establishment of NAFTA has eroded the non-reciprocal trade preferences the Caribbean receives from the US under the CBI. It also threatens investment diversion to Mexico. The attempts by the Caribbean to offset this through achieving parity with NAFTA have been stalled. They have also been complicated by the decision taken at the Summit of the Americas to initiate an FTAA in a relatively short timescale. The amount of preparatory work and negotiation to achieve this object will be immense. There are 26 regional and sub-regional free trade agreements to accommodate and while many of them do not directly involve the Caribbean, it has to be mindful of what is being decided elsewhere. It also has to define its own approach to the FTAA. A common approach is yet to emerge although one is being sought. The problem here will be similar to the one facing it regarding Lomé, but whereas negotiations with the EU are more structured and more known (as to both timetable and content) those for a FTAA are not, with the prospect that common positions will be more difficult to find.

The South Pacific

5.43 The South Pacific Forum (SPF), to which all the South Pacific small states belong, was formed in 1971. The SPF meets annually to consider a range of topics, including issues of development and regional co-operation. In 1995 the SPF adopted a Vision Statement and a Plan of Action setting out the way the South Pacific could adapt to the changing regional and international environment. Among the policy measures recommended were domestic reforms to improve competitiveness; trade reform, including reduction of tariff and non-tariff barriers consistent with the principles of the WTO; adoption and implementation of the investment principles agreed to by APEC as a means to attract investment from the Pacific Rim countries; closer regional co-operation in shipping and civil aviation; and the joint promotion of tourism. They also agreed to review existing patterns of trade, investment and other aspects of regional economic relations with a view to broadening, deepening and diversifying regional economic co-operation. This marked a renewal of interest in regional economic integration which had been a theme of early Forum activity but which was not taken up or developed in any purposeful way.

5.44 The South Pacific benefits from the Lomé Convention. The EU is a major aid donor to the region and instruments such as Stabex have provided valuable additional assistance. The Sugar Protocol is also vital to Fiji. However, the major extra-regional economic association is SPARTECA, concluded with Australia and New Zealand in 1980. This provides non-reciprocal duty free and unrestricted access to their markets for most raw products and for manufactured goods meeting a 50% or less rule of origin requirement. Although this has provided some benefits, the emerging view is that SPARTECA has not been particularly successful and that it has contributed to the development of uncompetitive industries in the islands. Accordingly, proposals have recently been trailed to establish an alternative Economic Association, the main aim of which is to provide a competitive investment environment. The Economic Association would encompass agreements on trade in goods and services; movement of private capital; movement of labour; and technical assistance. It would also be conditional in the sense that South Pacific members would pledge themselves to undertake reforms as set out in the 1995 SPF meeting in return for continuing economic assistance.

The Indian Ocean

5.45 Until very recently there has been very little development of a specific regional agenda for the Indian Ocean. The Indian Ocean Commission (IOC) was formed in 1982 and includes Comoros, Mauritius and the Seychelles. It outlined four areas of co-operation including economic and commercial activities. Some committees have been established and action has been taken on tuna fisheries, transport and tourism, but very little has been achieved by way of regional integration. In 1995, Mauritius hosted a meeting which resulted in the creation of the Indian Ocean Rim Association for Regional Co-operation (IORARC). The recently adopted Charter of the organisation focuses on trade facilitation, promotion and liberalisation; investment promotion; scientific and technological exchanges; tourism; development of infrastructure and human resources; and movement of people and service providers on a non-discriminatory basis. It is not intended that it should develop into a trade bloc, although the opportunities for preferential trade agreements among its members are enhanced.

5.46 The Maldives is a member of the South Asian Association for Regional Cooperation (SAARC). In 1993 a South Asian preferential trade agreement was signed which gives 'special and favourable treatment' to the least developed member countries. Mauritius and the Seychelles are in the Lomé Convention. Mauritius, in particular, has gained considerable advantage from Lomé through the Sugar Protocol and more particularly from the preferential treatment accorded exports of clothing to the EU.

Africa

5.47 Botswana, Lesotho and Swaziland were founding members of the Southern African Development Co-ordination Conference (SADCC) which was established in 1980. The original impetus was to provide a development framework avoiding entanglement with apartheid South Africa. That has now clearly changed. In 1992 a decision was taken to transform SADCC into the Southern African Development Community (SADC) and South Africa joined in 1994. Namibia and Mauritius are also members. SADC has become the major vehicle for regional integration in the region with a substantial sectoral programme and broad political and social aims as well as economic objectives. In 1996 a decision was taken to establish a free trade area among the twelve member states within eight years.

5.48 All the above, except for Botswana, are also members of the Common Market for Eastern and Southern Africa (COMESA) in which South Africa has observer status. South Africa's full entry into COMESA, which is a preferential trade area with plans for conversion into a common market by the year 2000, has wide ranging implications for the other members, most of whom are either small states or less developed countries, due to enormous disparities of wealth and power between South Africa and the others. There is also the problem of overlapping membership between SADC and COMESA which could lead to confusion and duplication of effort. A previous proposal to merge with SADC failed to gain support.

5.49 The Gambia is a member of the Economic Community of West African States (ECOWAS), established in 1975. ECOWAS sought to develop an ambitious programme of economic and social integration leading to the adoption of a customs union in 1990. This has not been realised and the future of ECOWAS has been put in some doubt by other proposals for West African integration.

5.50 The Lomé Convention is an important source of assistance for all the small African states. Under Title IV Botswana, Lesotho and Swaziland are classed as land-locked states which allows for special treatment to be accorded to them. The Gambia and Lesotho are also classified as least developed ACP states which provides additional support. The same classification is extended to Kiribati, Samoa, Solomon Islands, Tuvalu and Vanuatu. Specific provision also applies to island states and covers the Caribbean, the Indian Ocean and the South Pacific.

The Mediterranean

5.51 Cyprus and Malta signed association agreements with the EU in the early 1970s. These have brought substantial benefits to both countries, including greater market access and inflows of FDI which have supported diversification and development. These benefits, however, have been eroded by several recent developments including the establishment of the Single European Market, EU enlargement and the proliferation of similar agreements concluded by the EU with other neighbouring countries. The competitive advantage which both countries enjoyed was being lost to others, including Mediterranean regions within the EU which were able to claim substantial structural funds from the EU for economic development.

5.52 The decision to apply for full membership of the EU was taken on both political and economic grounds. Difficulties, however, have arisen for both countries which make early membership uncertain. In the case of Cyprus it stems from the continuing Turkish occupation of part of the country and a claim by Turkish Cypriots for permanent division of the island unless Turkey joins the EU at the same time. In the case of Malta, the new government elected in 1996 considered that Malta's economy had not developed adequately to take on the full burden of membership. The two sides are now expected to negotiate a new relationship short of full membership.

Small States and Regionalisation

5.53 Attempts at economic integration amongst developing countries in the past have centred around the promotion of free trade areas, import substitution at a regional level, and collective self-reliance. These attempts fell short of initial expectations. Intra-regional trade experienced slow growth; joint plans for industrialisation amongst groups of countries in a region failed, in part because of the relatively small size of markets and low levels of economic development; and political and economic policy differences slowed or destroyed attempts at joint action to implement sectoral programming on a regional scale or to control FDI. Trade liberalisation was either blocked or new tariff and non-tariff barriers erected. These negative experiences with attempts at regional integration among developing countries have not precluded new attempts at regional co-operation. The various sub-regional agreements point to a new attempt to co-operate. A feature of the 'new regionalism' is that while trade remains the core and central factor, agreements take fuller account of the prospects for co-operation in non-trade related areas, with a particular focus on the need to attract FDI. There is also a somewhat more realistic evaluation of opportunities and limits. The process of structural adjustment mounted by many countries has created more open and export-oriented and competitive economies. Successful outward and market-oriented policies have permitted countries to take advantage of regional demand for goods and services. In addition, the strengthening of the private sector and somewhat closer co-operation in the development of infrastructure have supported an environment in which new opportunities for trade have emerged.

5.54 The challenge posed by 'open regionalism' is beginning to be met by small states through the 'new regionalism'. However, two sets of factors, additional to domestic reform, are necessary to ensure that small states make a successful transition to new forms of regionalism. First a more innovative approach to regional co-operation amongst small states in a sub-region will be an essential element in the development strategies they adopt. Joint approaches to marketing, promotion of investment, procurement, infrastructure development, exploitation of EEZ resources, and the use of technology merit closer attention than has been the case in the past. Second, they need assurances from the international community that assistance and support will be forth-coming during the period of transition. The trade preferences now extended to them will need to be extended beyond the time horizon now contemplated. The IFIs will need to be more sympathetic to their need for finance by relaxing stringent rules of access to concessional resources and graduation. The major bilateral donors will need to maintain flows of concessional bilateral assistance while these states adjust. Such concessional assistance will need to be directed towards the strengthening of infrastructure, development of the human resource base, and support for protection of the environment.

5.55 The approach small states adopt will clearly depend on levels of development and the wider regional environment in which they are located. The problems are most acute for the Caribbean which will have to simultaneously deal with the US, the EU and with Latin America. The choices elsewhere are more limited but no less pressing. But what is clear is that the architecture of the new regional associations is likely to be radically different from that which is now, or until recently has been, in place.

Assessment

5.56 This chapter has evaluated the economic problems facing small countries and the adjustments which they will have to make to integrate into the global economy. The overall evidence is mixed. While some small states have indeed been successful in realising benefits from globalisation there are many small states that have not. It cannot be categorically concluded that size has been the determining factor given the fact that several small states followed their larger neighbours in integrating into the global economy. There is, however, some evidence to indicate that countries that embarked on domestic reforms were more successful. This leads to a view that policy rather than size has played a critical role. In this sense small countries appear to face the same set of choices as larger countries. This said, there is nevertheless a case that can be made in favour of the proposition that small states face handicaps that constrain them from embracing a full programme of reforms because of size.

5.57 At the same time, small countries, even though constrained, have little choice but to adopt a programme of reforms. The reform process must be gradual and pragmatic and take account of the prevailing circumstances. External support by way of access to concessional financial and meaningful transition arrangements must be in place to cushion the cost of reforms. Regional agreements will help to improve the competitiveness of many small states though their immediate effect is likely to be limited. However, there is no alternative to the implementation of reforms. Failure to act will marginalise small states and increase their vulnerability.

6

The Economic Dimension:
Response and Recommendations

6.1 The previous chapter drew attention to the urgent need for small states to undertake a number of reforms to improve their competitive position in the global economy. Most of them were inward directed with the principal task of creating and maintaining a stable macro-economic environment in which investment and the private sector can be encouraged. However, it was noted that the geographical region is an increasingly important arena for integration into the global economy and that, over and above this, small states must be pro-active in coping with challenges presented by the forces of globalisation. This chapter identifies three such challenges as the most immediate for all small developing states: the liberalisation of trade, improved marketing and resource mobilisation.

Trade Policies and Preferences

6.2 The major changes brought about by the liberalisation of trade and the emergence of regional trading arrangements have significantly altered the trade policy framework in which small states will need to operate in the future. While the Uruguay Round (UR) may have positive effects on small states in the long term, many of them are concerned about the transitional costs they face in adjusting to a freer international trading system. These will vary by country and by region depending on product, competitiveness and the degree of dependence on preferential access to major metropolitan markets.

6.3 The UR was launched under the auspices of the General Agreement on Tariffs and Trade (GATT) in 1986 and concluded in 1994. It is different from earlier multilateral trade negotiations by being more comprehensive in its scope and effect. Substantial reductions in most favoured nation (MFN) tariffs were agreed as well as the removal of a variety of non-tariff barriers. Estimates of the increase in global GDP from improved market access range from US$ 40 billion to US$ 315 billion annually, around one-third of which will accrue to developing countries. For most small states, however, as well as some larger ones in sub-Saharan Africa, the gains are expected to be small and some may even be net losers. While the figures have to be treated with caution, since overall increases in global trade may well increase demand for small states exports, the initial assessment is negative: Caribbean small states are expected to lose 3% of their export earnings per annum and South Pacific small states 1.1%. African ACP countries also face a 1.1% decline. Some of the countries which are likely to be significant losers are The Bahamas, Guyana, Jamaica, Kiribati, Mauritius, Papua New Guinea, Samoa and Trinidad and Tobago.

6.4 These anticipated losses are largely the result of reduced preferences. The reduction in MFN tariffs has also reduced the margins of preference small states have enjoyed under the Generalised System of Preferences (GSP) and the various regional preferential schemes to which they belong. In the case of the GSP schemes the impact is likely to be limited for two reasons: first, most small states receive more generous terms of access to their principal export markets under other schemes and second, the degree to which they can benefit from GSP is limited by a variety of restrictions and exclusions. The result is that small states are not significant users of GSP schemes and the proportion of their exports receiving GSP treatment is relatively low.

6.5 By contrast the other preferential trade schemes are very important. The major preferential trade schemes that benefit Commonwealth small states are the Lomé Convention, the CBI and SPARTECA. Since different rules govern their operation the best way to assess the effects is a sector approach.

Bananas and sugar

6.6 The two most important products which are likely to experience a negative effect are bananas and sugar. For CARICOM banana producers, especially Dominica, St Lucia, and St Vincent and the Grenadines, any reduction in preferences could have serious economic repercussions. The EU banana regime, under which these and other ACP countries are receiving a tariff-free quota, is under sustained attack by some Latin American banana exporters and the US and has been ruled illegal by the WTO. In addition, some EU member countries have questioned the legality of the scheme and with the accession of Austria, Finland and Sweden to the EU – all importers of low cost Latin American bananas – there has been increased pressure to amend the regime. Some changes have been introduced by the European Commission but these have not been sufficient to satisfy those opposing the regime and it is now almost inevitable that the regime will not be renewed in its present form when it comes to an end in 2002.

6.7 The small states in the Caribbean played an important part in the negotiation of the regime in the sense that they were able to put their views across, and to some extent get them acted upon, in the European

Commission and in several EU member states. The arguments they made then are still valid, but the negotiation of the regime was a difficult and protracted exercise which cost an enormous amount in time and resources for all concerned. The prospect of beginning again is daunting. The optimum position for the Caribbean small states is therefore a vigorous defence of the current regime over the next few years, combined with attempts at improvement in quality and price, to make their bananas more competitive with those from Latin America, although there are limits as to what can be achieved. The same applies to diversification. While it is imperative that the Caribbean banana producers make full use of the structural funds available under the European Development Fund (EDF) and take early steps to diversify their product base, the opportunities are limited. As yet no equivalent substitute has been identified in terms of economic and social welfare and resilience to hurricanes. These are considerations which point to bananas being an exceptional case to which exceptional measures need to apply.

6.8 Under the Sugar Protocol the EU guarantees to buy specific quantities from particular ACP states at an annually negotiated fixed price. In the past it closely followed the price guaranteed to EU sugar-beet growers. A number of small states have benefited significantly from this arrangement. A large fall in the EU internal price would be reflected in a lower price paid to sugar exporters. As a result of the agreement in the UR, a reduction in the price, of the order of 10%, is probable and would lead to a major drop in export earnings of sugar exporting countries. The most seriously affected would be Barbados, Guyana, Jamaica, Mauritius, Swaziland and Trinidad and Tobago.

Beef

6.9 The Beef Protocol is similar to the Sugar Protocol in that it provides specific quotas for export to the EU from specific countries for which exporters receive roughly the EU intervention price. Since the quotas are not fully used the main effect of liberalisation will be on export prices. A reduction of some 20% has been thought possible. Since 60% of Botswana's exports to the EU are beef the loss in earnings could be substantial. Smaller losses may also be experienced by Namibia and Swaziland.

Rice

6.10 Some ACP countries benefit from preferential access for their exports of rice to the EU. At present they receive a price roughly half-way between the world price and the intervention price paid in the

EU. As a result of the UR, a reduction in the prices of some 10% seems likely. The major impact will be on Guyana which has also been in dispute with the EU over access to its market for rice. In January 1997, at the initiative of the EU rice producing countries, the EU imposed safeguard measures which limit the export of rice into the EU from its Overseas Countries and Territories. This had the immediate effect of suddenly and substantially curtailing rice exports from Guyana and Suriname. There was no prior consultation with these countries, although this trade route had been legitimately used by them over a period of years.

Textiles and clothing

6.11 Under the UR the Multi-Fibre Arrangement (MFA), which has regulated the international trade in textiles and clothing, will be phased out over a period of ten years. Some ACP countries have taken advantage of the export restrictions imposed on Asian producers to develop a substantial export business based on tariff-free entry to the EU market. Caribbean exporters have also benefited from tariff advantages in the US market under the so-called 807A provision. Among the small states which have utilised these advantages to good effect to establish major export industries are Belize, Jamaica, Mauritius and St Lucia.

6.12 It is difficult to predict the pattern of trade in textiles and clothing that will emerge after the ten year transitional period. Even under MFA constraints the sector is unusual in that the product cycle is often as short as ten years. Preferential access and low labour costs attract foreign investment by producers from either the target market country or other developing countries which have had their access constrained. Sometimes the new producers themselves soon become subject to quotas (though this is not the case for ACP countries on the EU market) or their labour costs rise and/or alternative uses of labour become more attractive and the industry shrinks. Hence it is difficult to predict which countries will have a comparative advantage through low labour costs or higher productivity. Small states will probably continue to benefit from some advantages in tariff preferences in the EU and the US markets. Whether these will be high enough to maintain a competitive industry in the long run, however, is questionable.

Other products

6.13 A range of tropical products which in the past have been given favourable treatment, such as coffee, cocoa, and palm oil, will also be affected by the erosion of preferences. Even though the overall effects are likely to be small, some exporters in the Caribbean and the South Pacific are likely to lose market share. The same applies to some manufactured products which will face increased competition. Small states that are likely to be adversely affected include Botswana, The Gambia, Mauritius and Swaziland.

Other issues

6.14 The UR agreements also incorporated a number of new features. These include the agreements on TRIMs, TRIPs and the General Agreement on Trade in Services (GATs). The impact of these will in general be favourable even though it will necessitate major policy changes and some new costs. TRIPs, for example, is expected to lead to larger royalty payments but enhance access to technology. GATS, through the establishment of a sound multilateral framework, should impact favourably on countries which are exporters of labour intensive services. An indirect benefit would also follow from a reduction in the prices of services that small states purchase as inputs from the rest of the world.

6.15 The implementation of the UR agreements will make the multilateral trading system more orderly. The strengthening of existing rules and the establishment of more precise procedures will benefit small states. The reaffirmation of the principle of special and differential treatment for developing countries, the right to use import restrictions to support infant industries, while primarily designed to assist the least developed countries, will benefit some small states. However, the agreement on subsidies for non-agricultural products will prohibit the use of such instruments and will adversely affect middle income small states such as The Bahamas, Barbados, Cyprus, Jamaica, Malta, Mauritius, and Trinidad and Tobago. Some of the policy constraints arising from these agreements may not be entirely negative. Small states will also benefit from changes in the trading system that will be ushered in by the WTO regime in respect of anti-dumping and safeguard measures, non-tariff barriers and dispute settlement procedures.

Overall assessment

6.16 With further multilateral trade liberalisation and progressive decline in MFN tariffs expected, the scope of preferential arrangements such as Lomé will diminish over time. Small states will need to consider the future role of such arrangements. The priorities and interests regarding post Lomé arrangements may be different in each region, governed in the main by the structure and destination of its exports. The African states are largely dependent on EU markets and Lomé preferences are therefore important to them. For the South Pacific states, Lomé represents a limited benefit covering a small part of their exports. The circumstances of the Caribbean are more diverse and complex. The US market is the more significant market for many of the products exported by the majority of Caribbean states. However, for countries such as Guyana, Barbados, and the other Eastern Caribbean states, the EU is a major market for products such as sugar, rice, rum and bananas. Thus for the Caribbean, one or more of the preferential regimes offered by the EU and the US are important.

6.17 Small states will need to seek optimal arrangements in any new agreements that emerge after the expiry of the current Lomé Convention. As noted earlier, the European Commission has already published a Green Paper setting out some of the issues. The development problems for small states as a distinct group are not directly addressed at any point in it, though there are references to the particular difficulties facing the Caribbean ACP in respect of fashioning regional trade strategies and to problems peculiar to the small island economies of the South Pacific. This may be indicative of a preference for regional agreements. In this case small states will need to weigh up the pros and cons very carefully. The various regional fora need to be fully engaged in this process as well as the ACP Secretariat. The Commonwealth Secretariat can play a valuable role in the provision of technical assistance.

6.18 In the meantime the existing preferences in the EU could be more fully exploited. The financial and technical assistance resources available from the EDF for the promotion of ACP exports in global markets under the Trade Development Project should be more fully utilised. At the same time any relaxation of the rules of origin would provide tangible benefits for ACP countries.

6.19 Additionally, the Caribbean faces challenges from NAFTA. The advantages it had through preferential access to US and Canadian markets have been eroded with significant consequences for clothing and textiles and processed foods, particularly exports of orange juice and grapefruit juice. There will be two main effects. First, Caribbean exporters will face increased competition through lower prices for clothing and textiles manufactured in Mexico and for citrus fruit products. Second, new investment in the textile industry in the Caribbean is likely to suffer from diversion to Mexico as the result of its security of access to the US market and lower production costs, particularly labour costs. In addition, investment from other countries such as the EU could also be diverted to Mexico as a means of gaining entry to the US market. The countries most affected by these developments are The Bahamas, Jamaica and St Lucia.

6.20 The Caribbean has sought to counter the threat of NAFTA by seeking an interim parity agreement. However, there have been political difficulties in getting the proposed measure through the US Congress. The current US administration has promised to implement measures to increase Caribbean preferential access to the US through an improved CBI, but significantly a request for NAFTA parity received only token support. The US also rejected a request by Caribbean Heads of Government in early May 1997 to withdraw its opposition to the EU banana regime. This led one Caribbean prime minister at the time to be reported as commenting 'It must be clear to President Clinton and all his advisers that if the small Caribbean countries cannot live by trade in selling bananas to Europe and other goods to the US, then they will collapse and the region will become a playground for the narcotics cartels' (*Financial Times*).

Commercial and Marketing Policies

6.21 Many small states have recognised the need for diversification of their economies and have attempted to achieve that objective by encouraging private sector development activities. They have encouraged local and foreign entrepreneurs to invest while reducing the scope of their own involvement in the ownership of businesses by disinvesting. These governments have embarked on a programme of policy reforms and attempted to create an environment where the private sector assumes the role of an engine of growth. As exports have become more diversified, the need for further market development through a more dynamic and aggressive marketing strategy has become apparent. While joint ventures and transnational corporations have taken the lead and pursued their own marketing strategies, small and traditional domestic producers have been unable to mount similar efforts. Their expansion and diversification efforts have been constrained, largely because of their size and lack of sophistication. Studies have demonstrated the need for improved marketing arrangements. Some progress has been made. For instance, Geest boats can handle products other than bananas and the Eastern Caribbean Export Development Agency seeks to identify market opportunities in North America. However, the lack of funding in other areas has constrained the effort to promote and market other products.

6.22 Increased co-ordination and funding are needed in all areas of present and potential exports. While the private sector must bear the greater burden, a case can be made for public funding, especially for market information gathering and technical assistance in marketing. Past government efforts have not been particularly successful because of weak organisational arrangements. If governments are to be successful in a supporting role, they need to develop professionally competent and goal oriented organisations with strong links with private enterprises. Thus, a private–public sector partnership is essential.

6.23 Even with an effective orientation, many governments will still lack the means for launching successful marketing initiatives. These governments individually have limited financial and human resource capacities and are unable to 'go it alone'. Co-operative arrangements between several governments within a region do offer opportunities for the launch of successful joint programmes that enable potential markets to be turned into actual markets. This is important in all areas but particularly so in the tourism sector. Similar efforts in promotion of investment in a range of fields would also have large payoffs.

Aid Policies and Resource Mobilisation

6.24 A common characteristic of many small states has been the high level of dependence on ODA. High levels of ODA flows on a per capita basis to small states are unlikely to be sustained in the future and cutbacks will put strains on them. The decline in future ODA flows can be postulated on the basis of three emerging trends. In the first place the general aid fatigue and domestic policy concerns of the major bilateral donors have resulted in sharply reduced aid budgets. The US has reduced both its bilateral aid programmes and contributions to the IFIs. It has pledged a sharply reduced contribution to the next replenishment of IDA. The US actions have triggered lower contributions by other donors to multilateral aid programmes. These donors have also reduced their bilateral assistance. The second element concerns the intention of both bilateral and multilateral donors to channel resources to new claimants. These new claimants are either new member states in East and Central Europe, now in transition to a market economy, or countries and entities such as Bosnia, Croatia and the West Bank, that are emerging from prolonged periods of civil strife and are attempting a reconstruction of their devastated economies. Thus, the already reduced pool of ODA resources is being spread over a large number of countries. The third main theme of ODA policies is to assist the poorest of the poor countries, especially in Sub-Saharan Africa where poverty is overwhelming. Under these circumstances, small states are likely to see a reduction in the flows of ODA, particularly because of the perception that most small states are relatively well off.

6.25 While it is true that in most small states average income per head puts them into the category of middle income developing countries, per capita GNP is not a comprehensive, and therefore an altogether appropriate, indicator of development in small states. There are several reasons for this. One is these states' heightened vulnerability to internal and external shocks, both economic and environmental, which warrant the inclusion of an element of risk discounting in GNP calculation. Another is the higher unit costs per capita incurred from size in the provision of basic infrastructure and public services, which has already been highlighted. Third, the delivery of such services can be exceptionally costly, especially in the case of very small and remote communities in archipelagic SIDS, where duplication of provision is inevitable. The inescapable conclusion is that nominal income alone should not be used in determining the eligibility of small states for loans from IFIs.

6.26 However, access to these sources of finance is constrained by inflexible eligibility criteria. The IDA, the concessional resource arm of the World Bank, along with the Inter-American Development Bank (IDB) in its concessional lending, adopt a strict per capita GNP criterion for their credits, currently US$ 1,500 (1996 dollars). Accordingly, it appears that eligibility in 1998 will be confined to only 10 Commonwealth small states in the case of the IDA – The Gambia, Guyana, Kiribati, Lesotho, Maldives, Papua New Guinea, Samoa, Solomon Islands, Swaziland and Vanuatu – and in the IDB only to Guyana.

6.27 In contrast to IDA and IDB eligibility, the International Bank for Reconstruction and Development, another lending window of the World Bank, adopts a more flexible approach. Currently, it graduates out of its resources those countries with per capita incomes above US$ 5,435 (1996 dollars), with graduation usually occurring within five years of a country reaching the appropriate point. The decision to graduate is subject to two other important influences: access to capital markets on reasonable terms; and the extent of progress in establishing key institutions for economic and social development.

6.28 As noted earlier, small states are particularly disadvantaged in accessing international capital markets at reasonable cost. They also have difficulties in establishing stock exchanges to attract portfolio investment. As a consequence, it is difficult to believe that several Commonwealth small states which stand on the threshold of graduation (Antigua and Barbuda, Seychelles, St Kitts and Nevis) and others who may shortly follow, are as likely to meet the criteria as fully as other graduates of recent years (Ireland, Israel and New Zealand). In the case of small states, special considerations should apply.

6.29 It is our understanding that the Executive Directors of the World Bank have not considered for some years the special problems of very small economies (i.e. borrowing members with a population of less than 1.5 million) as a whole. In the past, the World Bank has recognised the special problems of small states, though it has not recommended any variation of the graduation policy. The time has come when existing policy should be reconsidered.

6.30 On their part, most small states will have to rely more on domestically generated savings than in the past. This will require governments to adopt fiscal policies which will generate increased public sector savings through surpluses. Private savings will need to be encouraged through improvements in financial markets where they exist, or through the development of institutions that will be capable of mobilising private savings. Fiscal policy will need to focus on constraining inflation, maintaining a stable exchange rate, and enhancing foreign competitiveness.

6.31 On the revenue side, small countries will need to broaden the tax base by reducing exemptions and concessions, and strengthening tax administration. Governments will need to curtail expenditure growth through measures that reduce the size of government, impose user charges for services and privatising government enterprises. Savings effected will need to be channelled into resources for infrastructure development in partnership with external financing sources.

Recommendations

6.32 The UR agreements and other changes in the international trading system pose major transitional challenges to small states. To benefit from them, **small states will need to re-orient their economies and diversify their production base.** They will need to strengthen the physical and human infrastructure in order to attract FDI flows. Sound macroeconomic management, a competitive exchange rate, and a dynamic role for the private sector will need to be in place. The international community will also need to respond appropriately to support the efforts of small states.

Trade policy

6.33 In the field of **trade policy,** Commonwealth small states would need to:

- assess and monitor changes in market access and identify new opportunities;

- eliminate any anti-export bias (i.e. high import duties which discourage export production);

- assess the rights and obligations of member states in the emerging global trading system, taking into account the special and differential treatment accorded to developing countries;

- review domestic policies, legislation and procedures to achieve conformity with the requirements of TRIPs, TRIMs and GATS;

- identify and introduce institutional and other support measures to enable the private sector to benefit from new trade opportunities.

6.34 In conjunction with these actions, governments will also need to undertake **new measures** to adjust to the changes brought about by the UR. Amongst the measures of importance are:

- ensuring greater use and exploitation of existing preferences under Lomé;

- increasing the awareness of the private sector to new market opportunities;

- improving competitiveness and product diversification;

- counter-balancing the erosion of preferences for particular product groups;

- investing in capacity building in the clothing and textile industry.

6.35 In respect of **new issues** in the UR small states should seek:

- the development of trade and labour intensive services within the context of GATS;

- to establish policy and institutional frameworks consistent with TRIMS to attract foreign investment;

- to promote accession to the WTO by those states who are not currently members.

6.36 These are major adjustments which small states will find difficult to realise without **external support**. One source is regional organisations. Many of the measures identified above can be co-ordinated regionally, particularly in negotiating changes in trade policy. The other source is the developed countries, especially those with which they have preferential trading arrangements. Small states must point out that it is in the interests of these countries as well as in their own interest that there is an orderly transition. They should therefore encourage them to take action in support of the reform programmes being undertaken. Among the measures which could be undertaken include:

- getting developed countries to provide fiscal incentives to their companies in order to encourage flows of FDI;

- elimination or removal of consumption taxes in developed markets to encourage imports of tropical products such as coffee and cocoa;

- encouraging more permissive 'rules of origin', not only in manufactures but also in fishing where the area of catch for 'originating' purposes could be extended to include the EEZ, in line with the UNCLOS.

6.37 IFIs, the EU and developed countries bilaterally can also devise **special regional development funds** for small states aimed at:

- identifying emerging trade opportunities for goods and services currently produced in small states or in which they might acquire a dynamic comparative advantage;

- the promotion of special projects to facilitate the transfer of production technology and marketing skills, as well as trade promotion.

6.38 Finally, the UR is likely to lead to an increase in prices for food produced in temperate zones. Since many small states are net-food importing countries this will lead to trade and welfare losses. The UR included a commitment by the developed countries, through the WTO, to consider providing food aid and/or compensatory finance from bilateral or multilateral aid programmes to the least developed and net-food importing countries who found themselves seriously affected. **The developed countries need to be reminded of their obligation to provide such assistance should it be needed.**

Marketing policy

6.39 Specific actions that ought to be taken in **marketing policy** are:

- a public sector role in gathering market data from the main markets, both present and potential;

- well financed joint private–public sector programmes in export promotion of both products and services;

- fiscal incentives to enterprises in the form of tax rebates against expenditures incurred in export promotion;

- joint government and private sector investment promotion missions to seek FDI flows.

6.40 At the **regional level**, joint intergovernmental trade representation would make a considerable contribution to economising resources. So too would joint trade and investment promotion efforts by the private sector and collaboration between the public and private sectors in these fields. For products common to several small countries in a region, a joint marketing and promotion effort should be established with cost sharing as an element for co-operation. Both traditional products, such as bananas and sugar, and services such as tourism should be covered by such arrangements.

6.41 Although a number of **international programmes of assistance** are in place to support product and market diversification (encompassing product adaptation, development of standards, export packaging, development of marketing skills, and marketing of tourism), the available resources are limited. **The bilateral and multilateral donor agencies should be urged to augment resources and earmark for these purposes.**

Resource mobilisation

6.42 The **mobilisation of domestic resources** through the appropriate fiscal policies, within the context of an overall macroeconomic policy framework that creates a competitive environment, will demand focused attention by governments. Governments will need to take steps to encourage private investment, both foreign and domestic. These steps will need to include an aggressive investment promotion effort and the removal of impediments to investment and any export bias. **Governments will need to make a strong case to donors for assured flows of ODA during a transition phase** in which they strengthen their capacity to mobilise both domestic and foreign resources.

6.43 At the international level, bilateral and multilateral donors should take a number of steps that contribute to national efforts. In so doing the **special position of small states** must be recognised. The vulnerability dimension must be taken into account along with the limited resources available to small states to implement the changes which are needed. The IFIs should reconsider their present approaches to determining eligibility to concessional lending by taking account of a broader set of criteria other than per capita incomes. We request Commonwealth Ministers to urge the **World Bank and the IDB to review their graduation policies and establish multiple criteria,** which take into account the special vulnerabilities and costs of its smallest borrowing member countries.

6.44 The development of **a robust vulnerability index** for the purposes sought by the 1995 meeting of the Commonwealth Ministerial Group of Small States (MGSS), namely 'to assist international consideration of the special problems of small states, including their access to concessional resources from international financial institutions', is essential to this exercise and should receive the highest priority.

6.45 Aid should be directed at **capacity-building,** both in terms of infrastructure and the development of human capital. Education and training should receive high priority. National financial institutions, donors and others should be encouraged to provide catalytic, equity financing schemes to assist in the development of a class of entrepreneurs who would strengthen the private sector. **A combination of capital and technical assistance should be targeted towards meeting the goals and objectives of the Barbados Plan of Action.**

Reform and the private sector

6.46 The pace of reforms needs acceleration in all states. **Small states that have yet to embark upon reforms need to do so as a matter of urgency.** Amongst the specific measures that are required are:

- a broadening of the tax base together with an elimination of customs surcharges and other taxes that have an anti-export bias;

- simplification of tax structures together with a strengthening of tax administration;

- an acceleration of the pace of privatisation of government-owned enterprises to increase efficiency, and use of the proceeds from the sale of public assets for investment in infrastructure;

- simplification of the regulatory framework aimed at encouraging private investment;

- provision of the necessary information to facilitate business decision-making;

- investment in development of the human resource base to underpin private investment.

6.47 Measures promoting trade and co-operation amongst a region's entrepreneurs, taking the form of business councils, regional Chambers of Commerce, product standardisation and sponsorship of trade and investment promotion missions is also likely to have a positive impact in **strengthening the private sector.** Indeed, a change in attitudes towards the role of the private sector, viewed as a full partner in development, is likely to make a significant contribution to enhancing the role of the sector and the prospects for sustainable development.

7

The Environmental Dimension: Analysis

7.1 Since the publication of the 1985 *Vulnerability* report, new concepts and approaches to economic development have become widely accepted as essential to conserve the environment as the common heritage of humankind. The 1987 report of the Brundtland Commission, *Our Common Future*, advanced a definition of sustainable development as 'development that meets the needs of the present without compromising the ability of future generations to meet their own needs'. This has been interpreted in practice as a commitment to a path of social and economic development which does not expose future generations to unacceptable risks, and that places considerable emphasis on improving the well-being of the poorest sections of society. Both aspects have pervasive implications for the development strategies of small states.

7.2 The 1992 UN Conference on the Environment and Development (UNCED), held at Rio de Janeiro, approved Agenda 21, which set out a comprehensive programme to achieve sustainable development worldwide. Chapter 17 addressed the special problems of SIDS, noting the combination of factors giving rise to vulnerability: small size, isolation from major markets, ecological fragility, geographic dispersion and limited resources. The 1994 UN Global Conference in Barbados adopted a specific Programme of Action to address these problems.

7.3 This chapter and the following address two elements of the environmental agenda for small states. The first is the issue of vulnerability. It examines the major risks to which small states are exposed and which can lead, in terms of our earlier discussion of threat, to a situation in which the quality of life of the inhabitants of a state is drastically degraded by a single act or event or a sequence of acts or events. The second theme is the adjustments that small states will need to make to their strategies and instruments for economic development if they are to achieve sustainable development.

Environmental Vulnerability

7.4 The environmental risks to which states are exposed can be divided into external and internal risks. The dividing line is not hard and fast, but the essence of the distinction is that external risks are 'imposed' by forces and events outside the state in question, while internal risks are generated within the state. The distinction does not rest on the degree of control over the risk: both external and internal risks may be open to control and mitigation by the state.

External Risks

Natural disasters

7.5 In 1990 the United Nations Disaster Relief Organisation (UNDRO) produced a report on the economic impact of disasters for 195 countries over the previous twenty years. Of the 25 most disaster prone countries, 13 were small island states. Some lost, in some years, between 28% and 1200% of their GNP. Several studies completed since then confirm that small states are likely to suffer disproportionately from natural disasters.

7.6 In 1995, Briguglio published a study using the data collected by UNDRO confirming that island states tend to suffer more in terms of per capita damage from natural disasters and damage per unit area than non-island states. In turn, small islands suffer more than large islands. The higher incidence of natural disaster on small island states tends to reflect their risk proneness and this in turn is a function of geographical location. Smallness also means that a given event, a volcanic eruption, is likely to have a highly concentrated level of damage, so that, in proportionate terms, more damage is done.

7.7 The Briguglio study is open to criticism. A number of island states are not in fact prone to hurricane or volcanic disaster. Countries with a zero score, i.e. zero risk, in the UNDRO list include Anguilla, The Bahamas, Barbados, Bermuda, Kiribati, Maldives, Reunion, Seychelles, Trinidad and Tobago, New Caledonia and Tuvalu (although the last two named have recently experienced cyclones). Nonetheless, if the UNDRO index is accepted it does suggest that small states are particularly prone to disasters. Taking the 'total' index (the total damage caused by disasters over 20 years divided by annual GNP), small states occupy five of the 'top ten' disaster prone countries, whilst on the 'average' index (total damage divided by the number of events to get a 'per event' damage indicator), small states comprise no less than eight of the top ten places.

7.8 A separate exercise, using the database of the Centre for Research on the Epidemiology of Disasters, which estimates the probability of a fatality, or of being affected significantly, by disasters also points out the risks in small states. While the data are imperfect, they suggest a lower risk of fatality from disasters in small states – about half that of the risk in large states – but a significantly higher risk of being affected by a disaster – about twice the risk in large states. This contrast arises partly because of the generally limited land area in small states, so that single disasters are likely to affect a greater proportion of the population. The lower death rate in small states perhaps suggests a greater state of preparedness in small states where disaster events are often familiar. A further complicating factor, however, is that the definition of disasters used in the database in question appears to include some civil conflicts. These can often raise numbers of deaths without necessarily affecting the whole population.

Vulnerability to sea-level rise

7.9 There is growing scientific evidence that human activity has begun to change the average temperature of the Earth's surface. These temperature changes have been brought about by the emissions of various 'greenhouse gases', most notably carbon dioxide from the burning of fossil fuels and from the burning of tropical forests, and methane, also from fossil fuel use and certain agricultural activities. The Second Assessment Report of the Intergovernmental Panel on Climate Change (IPCC) declares that 'the balance of evidence suggests that there is now a discernible human influence on climate' and 'the signal is just beginning to emerge from the noise of natural variability', but 'there are still uncertainties in key factors'. The global mean surface temperature of the Earth is expected to rise by $2°C$ by 2100 with a confidence interval of $1°C$ to $3.5°C$. Nor will warming stop in 2100 even if the concentrations of greenhouse gases in the atmosphere are stabilised: there are substantial time lags in climate change. Warming now is due to emissions of greenhouse gases in the past, the gases staying in the atmosphere for sometimes considerable periods before decaying. It is important to understand that the $2°C$ change is an average. There will be significant regional variations with some parts of the world experiencing less warming and some more.

7.10 One of the consequences of temperature change will be sea-level rise, mainly due to the thermal expansion of the oceans – the increase in the volume of water brought about by a temperature increase. The mean rise is projected by IPCC to be 50 cms by 2100, with a range of 15 to 95 cms. Other effects of global warming may be just as significant, notably the expected increase in the variability of weather: more storms and hurricanes, stronger monsoons, and so on.

7.11 Sea-level rise is of particular concern to small states as over half the countries classified as small states are islands. But, being an island is not the critical factor in terms of vulnerability to sea-level rise.

Many large countries have extensive coastlines that would be just as vulnerable, particularly when there are large population areas near the coast. However, the problem is especially acute for many small states as most populations, agricultural lands and infrastructures of SIDS exist in the coastal zone and for many the effect will also be felt on the marine environment with possible damage to coral reefs and to fisheries. There is also the danger of inundation of outlying islands and damage to vegetation and freshwater resources through saline intrusion.

7.12 The disproportionate risks small states face is set out in Table 7.1. This reproduces the survey in Turner et al (1996), but dividing countries into small and large states, and adding some new information. Crude averages offer some insights into the differential impacts. The survey did not include the two Commonwealth small states expected to be most affected by sea-level rise, namely Maldives and Tuvalu.

7.13 First, a far greater proportion of the population of small states suffers from the potential effects of sea-level rise than in large states, 66% against 9%. Notable are Kiribati and the Marshall Islands for having 100% of their populations 'at risk'. Absolute numbers are relevant in devising policies. In the 11 large states for which information is available, some 185 million people are estimated to be at risk from a one metre sea-level rise. In the seven small states for which data are available, the affected population is 800,000. Of course, one metre sea-level rise is not the final effect of unchecked global warming: sea-levels would continue to rise in the absence of effective policies.

7.14 Second, a similar picture is revealed for land area lost. Small states lose 1.6% of total land area while large states lose one half of this amount. If the USA is excluded from large states the percentages are much closer at 1.6% and 1.3% respectively. In absolute terms, the sample of eight small states lose just over 4,000 km², whilst the large states lose over 150,000 km², more than 35 times as much.

7.15 Third, capital value losses as a percentage of GNP are very large in Guyana and the Marshall Islands, with only one other small country having data showing this value. Losses in large states show a wide range with an upper bound of 200% in Egypt. Averages are not meaningful in this context but the general picture is one of capital losses being probably no worse in small states than in large ones.

7.16 Fourth, adaptation costs, defined as the costs of protection for all areas other than low population density areas, show a marked difference, although the sample for small states is small (five observations). It appears however that small states may face adaptation costs of some 2% of GNP per annum, with wide variation, compared to just 0.1% for large states. Turner *et al* (1996) suggest that large rich states already have sea protection systems in place that will cost modest amounts to improve (relative to GNP) whereas small states do not have such systems in place. The idea that the richer OECD states face less proportionate costs appears to be only partially borne out in Table 7.1. If Poland is included as a developed state, the average cost is 0.05% of GNP, but the example of Japan shows that costs can be very high even for rich countries.

Table 7.1 Impacts of One Metre Sea-Level Rise

Country	Population Affected (%)	Capital Value Loss as % GNP	Land Area Lost (%)	Wetland Loss km²	Adaptation Costs as % of GNP p.a.
Small States:					
Antigua	50	n/a	0.4	3	0.32
Belize	35	n/a	8.4	n/a	n/a
Guyana	80	1.115	1.1	500	0.26
Kiribati	100	8	12.5	n/a	0.10
Marshall Islands	100	324	80.0	n/a	7.00+
Mauritius	1	n/a	0.5	n/a	n/a
St Kitts and Nevis	n/a	n/a	1.4	1	2.65
Tonga	47	n/a	2.9	n/a	n/a
Big States:					
Argentina	n/a	6	0.1	1,100	0.02+
Bangladesh	60	5	17.5	5,800	0.06
Benin	25	12	0.2	85	0.41+
China	7	n/a	n/a	n/a	n/a
Egypt	9	204	1.0	n/a	0.45
India	1	n/a	0.4	n/a	n/a
Japan	15	72	0.5	n/a	0.12+
Malaysia	n/a	n/a	2.1	6,000	n/a
Netherlands	67	69	5.9	642	0.05
Nigeria	4	52	2.0	16,000	0.04+
Poland	1	24	0.5	36	0.02
Senegal	>1	14	3.1	6,000	0.21+
Uruguay	<1	26	0.1	23	0.12+
USA	n/a	n/a	0.3	17,000	0.03+
Venezuela	<1	1	0.6	5,600	0.03
Average					
Small States	66[1]	-	1.62[2]	-	2.0
Big States	9[1]	-	0.77[2]	-	0.1

The full list of studies on which these estimates are based is given in bijlsma (1996).

Notes: (1) numbers of affected people/total population
         (2) land area lost/land area

Source: Turner *et al* (1996) and consultant's calculations.

Vulnerability to extreme events

7.17 The second feature of climate change is likely to be increased frequencies of serious weather 'events'. Already some 45,000 people die every year in extreme events, mostly cyclones. Because cyclones can only form over hot sea surface temperatures they tend to be confined to certain areas, with particular risks to the small states of the South West Pacific and the Caribbean. Given a doubling of carbon dioxide concentrations, one estimate suggests there could be 8,000 additional deaths in the world from cyclones, and perhaps an additional US$ 630 million of damage. No detailed breakdown appears to be available to identify the extent to which small states would share in this projected incremental loss. Some caution is necessary in accepting these figures, particularly when a recent study on cyclones in the South Pacific reports no statistically significant increase in tropical cyclones between 1969 and 1994.

Marine pollution

7.18 The intensified use of oceans and seas as a resource for food, mining, energy generation, water, transportation, recreation and tourism have increased the importance of the marine environment and highlighted the need to control marine pollution. Oceans and seas have long been used as a 'sink' for waste disposal which can be either land-based (affecting mainly the immediate coastline through run-off and out-falls) or sea-based (through dumping or the passage of ships). While the former is the main source of contamination and pollution, marine transportation and the dumping of waste at sea account for nearly a quarter of pollutants entering the marine environment. These can take a number of forms ranging from potentially extremely hazardous items such as radioactive and toxic waste disposal to unsightly garbage and sewage disposal from passenger and cargo ships. Oil pollution is a significant problem for many states and can cause severe localised environmental damage.

7.19 In recognition of these problems a regional seas programme has been developed by the UN Environmental Programme which covers the Caribbean, the Mediterranean and the South Pacific. However, in all these areas considerable risks remain and in some instances these are growing risks. The increase in cargo and tanker traffic as a result of globalisation and of cruise ship tourism are two examples. A cruise ship with a complement of 1,200 passengers and crew will generate 4,200 kg of garbage per day exclusive of other pollutants such as oily wastes, residues and sewage. In the Caribbean, in the early 1990s there were on average 120 ships operating this trade while The

Bahamas alone received 108 visits per month. Ports in the region do not on the whole have the facilities to deal with the levels of waste generated by these and other shipping activities. Additionally, fears have been expressed that developing countries have been targeted by industrial nations as a dumping ground for hazardous waste and more generally that shipments of hazardous waste continue across their EEZs.

Internal Risks

7.20 Internal risks arise from the natural resource endowment of the nation state, the demands made on those resources, the human resources available, and the size of the market. Smallness seems likely to give rise to disproportionate risks since the availability of substantial resources is less likely, small populations limit available labour and entrepreneurship, and small populations similarly limit market size, thus preventing gains from economies of scale. In practice, the picture is more complex than this. Resource endowments are the result of a combination of features including land area, the chance of fortunate location, and climate. There need be no necessary correlation between population size and resource endowment. The examples of Namibia and Botswana show that natural resource richness can be accompanied by small populations.

7.21 Similar qualifications surround the concept of carrying capacity. In principle, any land or sea area has a limited carrying capacity, defined as the maximum number of people that can be sustained indefinitely with a given resource base. Traditionally, carrying capacity has been measured in terms of food availability, but other resource constraints may be binding, and indeed they may actually limit the level of population even before food constraints do. Obvious and relevant resources in the small size context are fuel supplies and water. Less obvious resources include the capacity of marine ecosystems, especially coral reefs, to sustain tourist activity. There is likely therefore to be a maximum number of tourists that can be sustained from given amounts of natural resources and amenity.

7.22 While the carrying capacity notion is attractive, it is important to understand its limitations. First, resource constraints are often capable of being relaxed through investment. The binding constraint might, for example, be summertime low level flow in a river. But that is capable of being relaxed through the construction of storage capacity which enables low flow augmentation. Second, the limits set by carrying capacity as far as any country or region is concerned can be relaxed through trade with other areas. A fuelwood deficiency might be reduced by importing fuelwood in exchange for something else. This avenue for relaxing the constraint, however, may not always be open and water is an obvious example of a commodity that is usually not traded in this way. Third, carrying capacity may change over time as demands on resources are reduced, perhaps through migration, and as the productivity of the resource base rises, perhaps through technological change. Nonetheless, investigating carrying capacity can be the source of helpful information.

7.23 This section examines some major examples of resource destruction and stress on carrying capacity – deforestation, desertification, freshwater provision, commercial fishing and tourism – which are directly relevant to small states.

Deforestation

7.24 Although the pressures for utilising indigenous resources in small states are likely to be high, there is little evidence to suggest that rates of forest conversion are any higher in small states than in large ones. Compared to the early 1980s, few small states show significant reductions in forest cover. Over 80% of the land area of the Solomon Islands is classified as forest and woodland, and there was just over 3% reduction of cover in the early 1990s compared to the early 1980s. Mauritius reveals the most dramatic deforestation rate for a small state, at 24% over the decade. Forest cover is now around 25% of the total land area of 200,000 hectares.

7.25 Typically, deforestation arises from a complex mixture of factors. Two dominant ones are rapid population change, either in terms of natural expansion or in terms of migration, and what might be termed 'economic failure'. Economic failure refers to the inability of economic systems to register the right market signals to capture the true economic value of environmental assets. For example, a forest has many ecological functions and these are also economic functions. They include the provision of timber and non-timber forest products (rattan, rubber, fruits, nuts etc.), the function of storing biological diversity, the protection of watersheds (such that deforestation often gives rise to flooding, river sedimentation etc.), and the storage of carbon which, if released through forest burning becomes the greenhouse gas carbon dioxide. Many of these functions have limited markets and some have no evident market at all. Thus, there is no obvious market in the carbon storage function, and no easy way in which those who benefit from watershed protection can pay forest owners or dwellers to conserve that function.

7.26 These 'missing' or 'incomplete' markets do much to explain why forest resources are undervalued relative to the alternative use of forest land, e.g. for agriculture and livestock. The choice of land use thus becomes biased in favour of so-called 'developmental' uses of forest land and against conservation and sustainable uses. Allied to this form of economic failure is another, sometimes called 'intervention failure' or 'government failure' whereby governments intervene in the workings of the economic system, often with very good motives, but to the detriment of forest cover. Many countries, for example, have subsidised forest clearance, a conspicuous example being Brazil in the 1970s and 1980s. Others fail to tax forest concessions at a reasonable rate, inflating the profits that forest concessionaires can achieve from clear cutting. Most pervasively, property rights in forest land are often poorly defined. This opens the way for new entrants to take land over, often to the detriment of indigenous peoples who may have traditional but unregistered rights to the land. Effectively, the forest becomes an 'open access' resource, not owned by anyone and abused by all. In other cases, open access becomes an invitation to claim the land regardless of any traditional rights that might prevail.

Desertification and soil erosion

7.27 There are a number of causes of desertification. They include overgrazing, overcultivation, woodland destruction and poor irrigation practices. These lead to an acceleration of processes already common in drylands such as soil erosion, resulting in significant environmental stress and reduced carrying capacity.

7.28 The small states most affected are in Southern Africa. They suffer moderate desertification defined as 25% or less loss in cropland productivity and livestock carrying capacity in rangelands. Pressures are severest in Lesotho where population growth and and an acute shortage of cultivable land has led to cultivation of former grazing land and unsuitable steep mountain slopes, leading to severe soil erosion. Poor pastoral practices have also added to the problem which has been further compounded in recent years by an above average incidence of drought. Botswana and Namibia also have major problems of soil degradation and overgrazing which have led to calls for better management of the important livestock industry in both countries.

Water

7.29 One measure of resource scarcity based on water availability is a simple water stress index which measures the per capita water availability for agriculture, industry and domestic use. The benchmark is 1,000 cubic metres per person per annum: below this level suggests that there will be problems. On this criterion six small countries are currently at risk – Bahrain, Barbados, Cape Verde, Djibouti, Malta and

Qatar. Some of the water stress states may well have both the technology and the financial resources to extract fresh water from sea water. Malta, for example, already does this on a significant scale.

Fishing

7.30 There is a global problem of overfishing. Current levels of harvesting of conventional marine resources are at or above levels which can be sustained. The pressures on fish stocks for food is increasing, reflecting both population growth in the developing world and higher demand for fish products. The rising real price of fish, along with the overcapacity of fishing fleets maintained by subsidy, are creating strong incentives to fish, leading to economic pressures on countries to limit the scope of national measures and international agreements to manage stocks sustainably. The Food and Agriculture Organisation (FAO) estimate that about 25% of the fish stocks for which data are available are overfished or depleted and that a further 44% are already either heavily or fully fished and at risk of being overfished.

7.31 The global statistics mainly reflect what is occurring within waters under national sovereignty and the problems of fisheries management are faced largely at this level. However, for many SIDS, it is also important to focus on regional and international management, particularly of straddling and highly migratory stocks which regularly cross EEZs and the high seas. Since the mid-1980s, an extra million tonnes of annual tuna catch has come mostly from the Western Central Pacific and Western Indian Ocean. The world catch of squids has also grown, with the coast of West Africa being a prime fishing location. The income that can be earned from licencing foreign vessels to access fish resources can be very significant and account, as in the South Pacific, for a substantial proportion of government revenue. There is therefore every reason to ensure effective regional management as established in the Forum Fisheries Agency and more recently internationally in the 1995 UN Agreement on the Conservation and Management of Straddling Fish Stocks and Highly Migratory Fish Stocks. The latter is particularly significant since it is the first time the precautionary approach has been applied in a high seas fisheries agreement.

Tourism

7.32 Small states figure prominently among nations that are heavily dependent upon tourism as a source of private and public revenues. Among the states where over 50% of export earnings come from tourism are Antigua and Barbuda, The Bahamas, Barbados, Maldives, St Kitts and Nevis, and St Lucia. To this can be added those who secure 20-49% of their export earnings this way: Belize, Cyprus, Dominica, The Gambia, Grenada, Jamaica, Malta, Samoa, Seychelles, and St Vincent and the Grenadines. Studies confirm that smaller states tend to have higher dependency on foreign tourism, and that there is an inverse statistical relationship between tourism receipts as a percentage of GNP and the population size of the country in question. This high dependency on a single source of revenue brings its own macroeconomic problems, but it also has a critical environmental dimension. If the number of tourists exceeds the carrying capacity for tourists, then the quality of the resource that sustains the tourist industry will itself decline. This will tend to deter repeat visitors and even potential first time visitors if they get to hear of the change in environmental quality.

7.33 Measuring tourist carrying capacity is notoriously difficult. One study suggests that small countries (defined as less than five million people) tend to experience a higher intensity of tourist demand per square kilometre, which in turn serves as an indicator for environmental demand. In small countries the demand amounted to 71 persons/km², just under ten in medium sized countries (5-30 million population) and just under one person/km² in large countries. Another study calculates that Bermuda had 142 visitors per km² in the daytime in 1990, compared to 18 for The Bahamas. The Cayman Islands had 17 persons/km² whilst some of the South Pacific islands (Fiji, New Caledonia, Samoa, Solomon Islands, Tonga and Vanuatu) had less, and sometimes substantially less, than one visitor/km². Even these numbers are difficult to interpret. Apart from the fact that different sources quote different numbers, congestion and environmental impacts may not be determined by the relationship between visitors and total land area, but between visitors and areas zoned for tourism. Some islands, for example, do not experience significant inland demand for tourism, whereas coastal zones can be heavily in demand.

7.34 Perhaps more important than numbers per km² is the fact that the relevant ecosystems are themselves very fragile. This is especially true of coral reefs. The other major determinant of environmental damage is land conversion for tourist resorts and/or tourist related economic activity. Land conversion for tourism has probably not been a significant factor in deforestation, since the demand for tourist land is primarily coastal resort based. But there is some evidence of wetlands being drained to create resorts. Studies of tourist behaviour suggest that they are very sensitive to the appearance of resorts in terms of both the general landscape and disamenity of beaches, and to the pollution of bathing waters. It has been suggested that falls in tourist numbers after 1987 in The Bahamas, Barbados, British Virgin Islands, US Virgin

Islands, French Polynesia and Bermuda may have been due to the effects of exceeding some generalised notion of carrying capacity, but the change in demand has not been subject to any analysis of the various factors that might explain it.

Ecological Fragility

7.35 One aspect of vulnerability to which much attention has been drawn in small island states is ecological fragility. Small islands act as habitats for species which are distant from alternative populations of the same species, and there is a high degree of species endemism. The introduction of other species threaten indigenous species which often lack the ability to compete with them and which therefore puts them at risk of extinction. The openness of modern economies means that this endemism is always at risk, and, indeed, islands have tended to be the focus of many of the recent species losses. There can also be economic consequences since many SIDS are developing ecotourism ventures exploiting the uniqueness of their species and habitats.

Vulnerability and Sustainability

7.36 The principal focus of this chapter is on vulnerability. But, as indicated in Chapter 2, vulnerability is also determined by the ability to withstand stress and shocks. The capacity to adapt and to be resilient can do much to lessen vulnerability even if not much can be done to reduce the incidence of risk. Actions taken by government are important here. While these must necessarily be specific to the risk or threat, the discussion at the beginning of this chapter introduced the idea of sustainable development. This links the environment and the economy together providing the frame-work within which specific action is taken. In assessing the vulnerability of a state, sustainability is an essential goal. An economy or ecosystem can be thought of as being sustainable if it possesses the capacity and capability to develop in a continuous fashion without the prospects for the future being threatened by the factors that give rise to the stress. In this way, the future well-being of a population is partly dependent on the resilience of the system, and that resilience depends in turn on certain features of the economic system. In the literature on sustainable development these features tend to be expressed in terms of the capital assets of the nation and their diversity. It is worth exploring, therefore, if small states have more or less of these 'sustainability features' than large states.

Sustainability indicators

7.37 To realise sustainable development any strategy of economic and social development should not seek to maximise gains for this generation if in so doing it reduces the capacity of future generations to provide for their own wants and needs. The capacity to meet needs depends on the stock of assets available to each generation. Call these assets 'capital'. Then the capacity of future generations to meet their needs will definitely be compromised if they have less of these assets than are available to the current generation. It follows that each generation should leave for the next generation a stock of capital assets no less than the stock it has available. This has come to be known as a 'constant capital rule', but a moment's reflection suggests that keeping the stock of capital assets will not be enough. Most countries have rising populations, and this is especially true in the developing world. Constant assets would therefore mean a smaller stock of assets per capita if population is rising. The rule needs reformulating to mean constant per capita capital stocks, and, of course, if future generations are to be better off than current generations, that rule should be further modified to mean at least constant capital, and ideally rising capital stocks. On this rule, population increase clearly makes the chances of achieving sustainable development less than if population is constant.

7.38 Offsetting this concern to some extent is the fact that capital can be made more productive in the sense that future generations should be able to secure more output and services from their capital stocks than the current generation does today. This is because capital tends to improve in efficiency over time, and the source of this increased efficiency is technical change. In turn, technical change comes about because of improved technologies and improvements in the management of technology. This immediately highlights the role of improvements in education, skills and the transfer of technology to small states.

Capital stocks

7.39 For sustainable development, then, we need constant or rising per capita stocks of capital assets, and, as a rough rule of thumb, we also require that the rate of technological change should at least offset, and ideally be greater than, the rate of population growth. But what is meant by 'capital'? It is very important to understand capital in its broadest sense. Traditionally, capital referred to man-made assets such as machines, roads, factories, houses, vehicles, and so on. As early as 1960, however, economists had begun to recognise that education was important in explaining economic development, so that the definition of capital was expanded to include human capital. It is only in the last decade that proper recognition has similarly been afforded to the environment as a source of economic development.

7.40 Environmental capital, or 'natural capital', comprises the full array of environmental assets, from oil and gas in the ground, to forests, the stocks of ground water and river water, the quality of the air, the quality and quantity of soil, and so on. At the global level these stocks include the atmosphere and its temperature regulating activities, the ozone layer and its role in regulating ultraviolet radiation, the various biogeochemical cycles that regulate hydrological and nutrient flows, and which provide the very life support systems on which we all depend.

7.41 Today, there is also interest in the final constituent of the capital concept – social capital. Social capital is what holds society together, what gives it cohesiveness. Without social capital, social regulation breaks down and one can expect more crime, public disorder, family breakdown, drug abuse etc. This is a new area of investigation and little can be said in specific terms about the role of social capital in the development process. However, we have earlier identified cohesiveness as an important characteristic of many small states and anything which can be done to improve it is a factor contributing to resilience and reducing vulnerability.

7.42 The constant capital rule requires that the total stock of capital per capita – man-made, human, and natural – be at least constant through time. Efforts to measure this total stock have only just begun. A World Bank study in 1995 provides some preliminary estimates. The most important observation on small states is that they are neither among the richest nor the poorest states in the world. Only two (Suriname and The Bahamas) have a per capita wealth above US$ 200,000 compared to 26 large states and only ten (among them The Gambia, Kiribati, Maldives and Samoa) have a per capita wealth less than US$ 25,000 compared to 70 large states. Most small states have per capita wealth in the range US$ 25,000 to US$ 199,999.

7.43 It must be emphasised that such estimates are not especially reliable since they are based on inadequate data and have only been collected for one year. They should therefore be regarded with considerable caution. As far as small states are concerned, the implications are mixed. In so far as most of them are middling states they are unlikely to be targeted by external donors funding poverty reduction programmes designed to achieve sustainable development. On the other hand, the environmental risks to which small states are exposed, especially SIDS, would appear to suggest higher margins of per capita wealth are needed if they are to seriously reduce vulnerabilities across the board. Equally, the above average per capita income levels enjoyed by many SIDS provide an important cushion for coping with the impact of natural disasters and the wide fluctuations of national income which trouble many of them.

8

The Environment:
Response and Recommendations

8.1 Most small states are island developing states and middle income developing states. Both these features bear significantly on how they cope with the environment. The international community has recognised that SIDS are particularly at risk. A number of programmes and initiatives have been launched in the last ten years designed to reduce their vulnerability and improve their chances for sustainable development. These have met with mixed success and while there have been significant improvements many problems remain. Much of this has to do with resources, or rather the lack of them. Small developing states as small states and as developing states frequently lack economic capital, human capacity and technical skills, yet this double burden is too often unrecognised by the international donor community who are prepared to extend additional finance only to the least developed amongst them. Small states therefore necessarily and increasingly will have to look to their own resources to manage the environment.

8.2 The focus of this chapter is on how small states can cope better with a wide range of environmental challenges through appropriate policy responses, including more effective integration of economic and environmental policies. It also considers how suitable policies at international and regional levels can assist the sustainable development of small states.

The Special Problems of SIDS

8.3 The special circumstances and needs of SIDS are recognised in the 'Programme of Action' adopted by the UN Conference on the Sustainable Development of Small Island Developing States in 1994. The Programme addresses the sustainable development of SIDS in a comprehensive manner and proposes numerous measures which should be taken at the national, regional and international levels. Specific sections deal with climate change and sea-level rise; natural and environmental disasters; management of waste; coastal and marine resources, fresh water; land resources; energy; tourism; biodiversity; national institutions and administrative capacity; regional institutions and technical co-operation; transport and communications; science and technology; human resource development; trade; and financial resources.

8.4 The Conference agreed that the UN Commission on Sustainable Development (CSD) would monitor the programme as part of its work. At their June 1997 meeting, Commonwealth Environment Ministers expressed disappointment that little progress had been made in the implementation of the Barbados Programme. A comprehensive review of the Programme is to be undertaken by a two-day special session of the UN General Assembly in 1999 (immediately preceding its annual session).

8.5 Several small states could be the front-line victims of the consequences of global warming which has been caused by the policies and actions of larger countries. Commonwealth Environment Ministers have agreed that this critical issue requires urgent global response. The scientific projections have underscored the importance of implementing existing commitments of industrialised countries under the Climate Convention and reducing emissions beyond the year 2000. Different approaches have been proposed for this purpose. Some emphasise the need to adopt legally binding targets for uniform reduction of emissions of greenhouse gases by industrial countries, while others stress the need for an agreement to be fair, achievable and realistic. It is vital to promote consensus on this issue in order to reach agreement on effective measures to reduce global warming and sea-level rise at the Kyoto Conference of Parties to the Climate Convention in December 1997.

8.6 Three areas which demonstrate the difficulties involved are sea-level rise, natural disasters and tourism. As noted in the previous chapter, climate change and associated sea-level rise is a general problem for many small states and an acute problem for some SIDS. The need for action is both urgent and expensive. The same goes for natural disasters which are the single largest immediate external risk to many SIDS. Much can and has been done to mitigate their effects but the costs remain considerable and more can be done to share the burden internationally. Tourism was also identified in the previous chapter in the section which discussed internal risks. It offers significant development benefits to small states if it is managed sustainably, but efforts in this direction have only just begun and in some SIDS there is a considerable legacy of problems to overcome.

Reacting to sea-level rise

8.7 While it is imperative to slow down global warming by reducing greenhouse gas emissions, it would be prudent for the most vulnerable small states to consider policy options for coping with sea-level rise. These tend to be classified as 'retreat', 'accommodate' and 'protect'. Retreat basically means relocating activity away from areas at risk and allowing inundation to occur. While this may not seem logical at first, it can be the most sensible policy in circumstances where the costs of other forms of action greatly outweigh the value of the resources at risk. 'Accommodate' means adapting to sea-level rise, for example, by raising buildings above the ground. 'Protect' will primarily mean building up sea defences. Actual policy is likely to be a mix of all three options: some land will not be worth saving, for some people and some activities relocation will be most preferred, but clearly there will be contexts in which only prevention will make sense. This would be the case for those countries where most (or even all) of the land area is at risk. IPCC (1992) estimates such protection costs (last column of Table 7.1) and these are seen to vary widely. The Marshall Islands, for example, would have to spend 7% or more of its annual income on protection measures to bring risks down from 20,000 people being affected to 2,000. St Kitts and Nevis would also face a major bill of nearly 3% of GNP (as a benchmark, industrialised countries tend to spend 1.5-2% of their GNP on environmental protection generally). Other small states, however, could protect most of the population at risk for expenditures that are comparable to those for larger states.

8.8 IPCC (1992) reports further vulnerability indicators for more aggregated regions. This is convenient for current purposes since the classifications include island states. Table 8.1 shows developing country regions with above world average risk factors in terms of percentage of populations at risk.

Table 8.1 World Region Risk Factors for Sea-Level Rise

Region	People at Risk as % Population		Cost as % of GNP p.a.
	without protection	with protection	
Indian Ocean small islands	21.5	2.3	0.74
Atlantic Ocean small islands	10.8	1.2	0.09
Caribbean islands	9.5	1.1	0.19
Pacific Ocean small islands	6.8	0.8	0.73
Middle East	5.5	0.8	0.03
South Asia	4.2	0.5	0.10

8.9 The most notable feature of these estimates is the high proportion of people at risk in Indian Ocean small island states – 22% of the population. This can be brought down to just over 2% of the population at a fairly considerable GNP cost. In a similar fashion, South Pacific small islands can secure a tenfold reduction in the population at risk for a fairly sizeable expenditure.

8.10 How far the expenditure figures shown here are proper indicators depends on the extent to which the retreat and accommodation options have been built into the estimates, i.e. protection will not necessarily be the best option. But, clearly, some island states have no option. Nor, of course, would such states necessarily bear the costs of protection wholly themselves as some form of international aid can be envisaged.

Natural and environmental disasters

8.11 A number of initiatives and programmes have been developed in both the Caribbean and the South Pacific which have significantly improved disaster mitigation, preparedness and emergency relief management. The Caribbean Disaster Emergency Response Agency co-ordinates disaster relief in the region. At national level many states are undertaking disaster reduction activities supported by the Caribbean Disaster Mitigation Project, which is funded externally. A similar programme in the South Pacific is the South Pacific Disaster Reduction Programme which provides a framework for regional co-operation and exchange as well as support for national disaster management. Elsewhere there is little progress to report and much remains to be done.

8.12 Everywhere, national efforts remain critically underfunded and only a few countries have established national emergency funds. This leaves SIDS unnecessarily exposed and dependent on regional and international action. Recent experience in the Caribbean indicates that the lack of emergency funds and effective procedures for emergency disbursement slows down the delivery of assistance from national and international agencies. Yet few countries there or in the South Pacific regard such funds as priority. They need to be established where local circumstances permit along with appropriate national insurance pro-grammes with governmental and private sector participation. The mobilisation of international funds as part of this effort is critical but likely to be difficult. Other national measures which have been identified as important for reducing the impact of disasters are institutional development, including early warning systems and human resource development for disaster management; the integration of natural and environmental disaster policies into national planning; and the improvement of systems and arrangements for information and com-munication.

8.13 Disaster preparedness and mitigation at a regional level is regarded as particularly effective. It is this level which can best assess risk and vulnerability, identify common interests and requirements, and develop co-operative mechanisms to assist in disaster relief. Examples include early warning systems, the sharing of expertise and the development of standardised legislation such as the Caribbean Uniform Building Code which has improved hurricane resistance in the built environment. It is therefore important that existing regional disaster reduction mechanisms in the Caribbean and the South Pacific be strengthened and consolidated and that regional co-operation be encouraged elsewhere, for example in the Indian Ocean.

8.14 The further development of national and regional programmes demands significant levels of international support. The Yokahama Strategy and Plan of Action adopted at the World Conference on Natural Disaster Reduction in 1994 recognised the need to pay special attention to the vulnerabilities and needs of SIDS. However, many SIDS argue that little has been done to mobilise the additional financial resources required for a comprehensive programme of disaster reduction. They also point to the urgent need for international action to provide access to technology, training and information over a range of activities. It is difficult to escape the conclusion that more should and can be done by the international community to support their efforts in disaster reduction programmes.

8.15 Finally, the Commission on Sustainable Development (CSD) in a recent report note that 'the potential danger posed by the frequent passage of commercial vessels, and on occasion vessels carrying toxic and hazardous wastes through the high seas surrounding a number of SIDS continues unattenuated'. The dangers of marine pollution and of the transport of hazardous waste have been identified earlier. The signing of the Waigani Convention covering the South Pacific and the statement issued by the Heads of Government of CARICOM in 1995 on this subject indicates the importance which many SIDS now attach to this matter. Questions concerning the transboundary movements of hazardous and nuclear waste are under active consideration in other fora such as the International Atomic Energy Agency. Since the current state of international law in this area is unclear and there are divergent views and practices among different countries, the international community needs to develop more effective instruments and arrangements which address the concerns of small states.

Sustainable tourism development

8.16 Tourism has had a significant economic impact on most SIDS. It has accelerated the growth of national income, boosted foreign exchange earnings, provided labour-intensive employment opportunities, and contributed to government revenues. Tourism and tourist-related activities have become the mainstay of the economy in many Caribbean and Indian Ocean SIDS while elsewhere it is a major or growing sector of activity as in the Mediterranean and South Pacific SIDS. The prospects for future growth are good with forecasts suggesting that between 1995 and 2005 travel and tourism will grow by an average annual rate of 5.5% in real terms, outpacing the growth of world economic output.

8.17 Many SIDS are well placed to capture a share of this market. They will, however, have to integrate tourism into their development programmes more carefully than they have done in the past. This is not simply an economic question but also a social and environmental one. The rapid development of mass tourism can put significant pressures on SIDS. The number of visitors at peak periods can exceed the local population in the smaller SIDS and in larger ones there can often be localised carrying capacity problems as tourists crowd beaches and roads and command local amenities. There can also be fall-out from crime and drugs.

8.18 The principal environmental difficulties have been identified as pressures on land resources and wildlife; limited infrastructural facilities to deal with solid and liquid waste generated on land and at sea; coastal area degradation affecting beaches, mangrove forests and coral reefs; and intensified use of scarce freshwater resources. These, along with the generalised problem of the effects of climate change and sea-level rise, pose major problems which, unless sustainably managed, could undermine and destroy both local communities and the tourist economy.

8.19 The interrelationship of the economic, social and environmental impacts of tourism mean that any plan for sustainable tourist development needs to be comprehensive. There have to be policies and measures to enhance the economic benefits from tourism as well as to ensure that tourism is socially and culturally acceptable. The greater involvement of nationals in the tourist sector can do much to ensure both outcomes. In relation to the environment careful vetting of tourist development proposals is needed along with the use of economic instruments to recover costs such as user fees for national parks; charges on the tourist industry for water and waste management; and the review of taxes and elimination of subsidies which have environmental costs. The fact that in many SIDS the private sector is alert to and aware of the need for sustainable development as sound business practice is a bonus and support for such measures. There is also a case for further enactment and improved enforcement of environmental legislation.

8.20 Benefits can also be gained by collaboration among SIDS at the regional level and international levels. In both the Caribbean and the Pacific regional tourism bodies have been established to strengthen tourist development, planning and promotion. The latter is particularly important given the costs of overseas marketing and can lead to significant economies of scale being realised. A regional conference on sustainable tourism has been held in the Caribbean and is planned for the South Pacific. Another initiative taken in 1995 was the World Conference on Sustainable Tourism which adopted a 'Charter for Sustainable Tourism' and a programme of related activity to follow up on its work. The UN system has also sponsored a number of initiatives in support of such activity in recent years.

Financial resources

8.21 The Barbados Programme of Action recognises that the increased significance attached to the sustainable development of SIDS will require the provision of 'adequate, predictable, new and additional financial resources' in accordance with Chapter 33 of Agenda 21. It also calls for more efficient use of official development assistance and other sources of external finance; greater co-ordination of the efforts of donors and recipient; exploration of the use of innovative financing mechanisms; the provision of concessional finance and technical assistance at levels necessary to the support sustainable development of SIDS; and targeting such assistance where it is most needed. The Programme also urges SIDS to ensure their macroeconomic policies are supportive of national sustainable development goals and priorities, and to mobilise additional supportive domestic resources by promoting private sector investment and exploring the increased use of economic instruments and innovative financing mechanisms.

8.22 The macroeconomic dimension is examined in the next section. In respect of external finance there is considerable uncertainty, and hence concern, as to whether sufficient resources will be forthcoming. The record to date is not encouraging. Overall, financing for implementation of the Programme of Action through bilateral or multilateral resource flows has declined over the period 1991–94. While bilateral flows have predominated they have been concentrated in a relatively few countries (for example Haiti and Palau) reflecting US political priorities and established patterns of commitment (assistance from Australia and New Zealand has gone overwhelmingly to South Pacific SIDS and Canadian assistance to Caribbean SIDS). In terms of the 14 priority areas identified in the Programme, external resources have been channelled predominantly to human resource development, national institutions and administrative capacity, transport and communications, and land resources. Natural and environmental disasters and tourism development have received modest sums at best and climate change and sea-level rise none at all.

Macroeconomics and the Environment

8.23 The Langkawi Declaration on the Environment adopted by Commonwealth Heads of Government in 1989, drew attention to the need to integrate economic and environmental policies in order to make development environmentally sustainable. This was also emphasised in Chapter 8 of Agenda 21. Essentially, economic instruments are designed to influence the costs and benefits of alternative action open to economic agents. In contradistinction to command and control approaches, economic instruments rely primarily on incentives and market stimuli to produce desired outcomes. When properly deployed their effect is to influence behaviour in such a way that alternatives are chosen that lead to a more environmentally desirable situation than would obtain in the absence of such instruments.

8.24 In this section the role of such instruments is examined. The focus is on new and innovative sources of finance to raise revenues. These include inward looking measures that price the environment and outward looking measures that capitalise on the environmental assets that small states possess.

Macropolicy reform

8.25 The focus on sustainable development is appropriate for all countries, but especially so for small states. Many small states have significant 'environmental sectors', in the sense that they have non-renewable natural resources, such as minerals; renewable natural resources such as coral reefs, fisheries and wildlife; natural resources which are mixtures of renewable and non-renewable elements such as beaches and wetlands; or a desirable climate. All of these, climate included, can be lost through the act of capital depreciation – of running down such assets without taking care to renew them. Depreciating environmental assets may occur because of domestic policy, because policies are imposed on a small state externally, or because of some global change which threatens the small state environment, as with global climate change.

8.26 Underlying this emphasis on the natural environment is the idea that economy and environment interact. The idea that economic activity has impacts on the environment is of course not new: it underlies, for example, the early discussions on 'Limits to Growth'. What is less well appreciated, however, is the extent to which environmental damage impairs economic performance. For example, estimates of the economic cost of air pollution damage in terms of damage to human health in large cities like Cairo, Bangkok and Jakarta ranges from US$

30 to US$ 400 per capita. The fact that such damage only partially appears in the conventional GNP accounts underlines the need for better indicators of human welfare change. But it also suggests that the dependence of economy on environment would be better revealed and understood if such indicators were adopted.

8.27 Once the interactions between the economy and the environment are understood, our appreciation of macroeconomic policy also changes. It is customary to think of macroeconomic policies as including management of the major macro-variables influencing the economy – exchange rates, interest rates, and government budgets. But macropolicy also includes the liberalisation of domestic markets and international trade, privatisation and pricing reform. Substantial experience has now been built up on the links between changes in these policy variables and the environment and while considerable uncertainty remains because interactions are often complex it is nonetheless true that certain general results can be formulated.

8.28 First, it is generally, though not universally true that price reforms will both improve the chances of economic progress and help the environment at the same time. Second, reforming one policy variable without attending to the distortions in others tends to be counterproductive. Reform has to be 'across the board'. Third, stability may matter as much as the general trend of change. Macroeconomic stability – the avoidance of severe fluctuations in policy variables – leads to more stable expectations which in turn encourage sustainable resource use rather than the rapid 'mining' of resources because the future is uncertain. Consistency of policy as much as the policy itself matters. Fourth, macropolicy changes can benefit long term economic growth and employment. Contrary to the 'limits to growth' literature, these outcomes can benefit the environment as wealthier populations demand higher environmental quality, and, probably more important, as reductions in unemployment reduce the pressures on 'free' resources such as fuelwood.

Demonstrating and Capturing Environmental Value

8.29 Pricing is central to macropolicy reform. Pricing natural resources properly is a form of 'value capture': economic value resides in environmental assets but that value is all too often not reflected in the market place. By creating and extending markets in these assets, the latent economic value is released and captured. The two stages of environmental pricing reform are therefore known as 'demonstration' and 'capture': the former is the exercise of showing that economic value exists, the latter is the process of ensuring that this value accrues to the relevant parts of society.

Demonstrating economic value: resource accounting

8.30 Placing economic values on environmental assets is controversial but essential for sustainable development. For as long as environmental assets do not have economic values ascribed to them, their true importance in economic decision-making will be neglected. The process of demonstrating economic value involves specialised techniques of economic valuation, and these techniques can be applied at the micro-scale to assist in making decisions about, for example, whether or not to permit a coastal development; or at the macro-scale to reflect better the economic value of environmental assets in the national accounts (GNP). The former activity of resource accounting is encompassed in cost-benefit analysis. The latter involves national resource accounting to include environmental depreciation of assets to arrive at 'true' or 'green' net national product. Reforming the national accounts in this way is urged in Agenda 21.

Table 8.2 'Green' National Accounts for Papua New Guinea

(10 million kina)

	1986	1987	1988	1989	1990
Net domestic product (NDP)	2,314	2,569	2,862	2,698	2,760
less					
Depletion of resources +	145	228	124	43	199
Quality degradation	36	36	36	36	36
Total depreciation	181	264	160	79	235
equals 'green' NDP	2,133	2,305	2,702	2,619	2,525
Environmental depreciation as % NDP	7.8	10.2	5.6	2.9	8.5

For each year, the adjustments shown are for depletion, i.e. the running down of stocks, and 'quality degradation by residuals', i.e. pollution. For resource depletion the approaches varied but included multiplying physical stocks changes by the 'rental' value of the resource (essentially, price minus cost of extraction). For pollution damage the approach used was to value damage at the cost of avoidance or restoration. This is not theoretically correct but reflects the difficulties of obtaining estimates of the monetary valuation of damage actually done by pollution.

Source: adapted from Bartelmus et al., 1993.

8.31 A number of studies have taken place on 'green' national accounting. Table 8.2 reports the only existing study for a 'small' state as defined in this report, Papua New Guinea. It shows that environmental depreciation ranges from 3% to 10% of Papua New Guinea's net domestic product. It is not obvious if this makes Papua New Guinea unsustainable or not. Papua New Guinea, after all, has substantial natural resources. In countries which are not so well endowed such levels of depreciation could be unsustainable. To have general effect and to be really meaningful, 'green' national accounting would need to be adopted by all countries.

Capturing economic value: pricing the environment

8.32 A central feature of the studies on macropolicy and the environment is the emphasis they place on price reform. Reform can be thought of as a two stage process: first, cost recovery, and, second, charging for environmental externalities. Cost recovery means raising prices so that they at least cover the (marginal) costs of production. Externality charging means raising prices further to reflect the use of environmental resources not included in market prices.

8.33 Subsidies have a number of distorting effects. First, they send the 'wrong' signals to users of a resource. By keeping prices low, resource use is encouraged. Examples of over-use because of low cost recovery are widespread and include pesticides, resulting in excessive application rates and risks to those handling the chemicals; irrigation water, the excessive use of which can give rise to waterlogging and salinisation; fertilisers, resulting in excess runoff into watercourses and increased nutrient content of water (eutrophication); fossil fuel energy, resulting in unnecessary air pollution and waste of resources. Second, producers are encouraged to oversupply the market in order to meet the excess demand arising from low prices. At the same time, they have no incentive to be efficient in the production of, say, energy since the more they produce the more subsidy is received. Indeed, output may be exaggerated in order to collect larger subsidies. Third, the subsidy has to be paid for through some other form of financing. The result is either an excess tax burden on other industries and households, or, if tax rates are thought to be 'fair', the loss of some other benefit that could be obtained by spending elsewhere the money absorbed by the subsidy.

8.34 Subsidy removal in developing countries has progressed, although evidence on subsidies in small states seems to be missing. None of the case studies included in the World Bank programme on economy-wide policies and the environment is a small state and the same is true for the case studies produced by the Asian Development

Bank. It would be surprising, however, if the lessons were any different for small states. One obvious problem in reducing subsidies is the effects on the poor. One study evaluating these impacts in six large states (Colombia, Ghana, Indonesia, Malaysia, Turkey and Zimbabwe) finds that energy subsidies tend to benefit the non-poor urban households. They found only modest effects on industry and significant benefits on public budgets, suggesting that any impacts on poorer households might be offset by the savings in public expenditure.

8.35 The second stage of price reform is the pricing of goods and resources to reflect their 'full cost', including the cost of environmental services. This is the essence of the 'polluter pays principle' whereby the costs of achieving any given environmental standard are, in the first instance, met by the producer of the good or extractor of the raw material. Some of this increased cost will be passed on to consumers and it is important that it should be since consumers also need to receive the right 'signal' that a good has a high or low pollution content. The ways in which these full costs are charged to products is through environmental taxes and tradeable permits. The full costs of using a natural resource can be recovered through resource charges.

8.36 Environmental taxes and resource charges can be considered together. The principle is the same: a price is charged for the use of a scarce environmental asset, whether it is a clean atmosphere, river quality, or a wildlife reserve. Taxes and charges may take various forms: the product may be taxed directly – a product charge; or it may be possible to tax the polluting emissions directly, an emissions tax; or the use of the resource is subject to a resource charge. In turn, emissions taxes may be directly related to emissions or to the ambient quality of the environment (i.e. damage done as opposed to emissions). Contrary to popular opinion, environmental taxes, sometimes known as 'ecotaxes', are widespread. In several Scandinavian countries between 6% and 11% of total tax revenues derive from such taxes.

8.37 Examples of tax/charges in developing countries include Congo's tax on the clearing of public forest land, Malaysia's effluent charge system, and Kenya's policy of charging entry prices to wildlife game parks. Taking the last example, the power of proper pricing is noteworthy. First, Kenya deals with a great many tourists each year, but questions have been raised about the extent to which wildlife tourism and some hunting constitutes the best use of scarce land resources. It has been estimated that Kenya forgoes some US$ 200 million per year in agricultural output because of wildlife conservation. When due allowance is made for the role played by beach resorts in tourist revenues, repatriation of profits to other countries, and the costs of supplying the tourist trade, Kenya may be making only US$ 40 million net profit from wildlife. But the apparent relative unprofitability of wildlife reflects a failure on the part of Kenya to capture the full economic value of wildlife. Other studies show that tourists are willing to pay around US$ 400 million per annum to ensure wildlife viewing. One simple capture mechanism is to raise the entry prices to game parks. This would be a self-defeating measure if demand was very responsive to price – demand would fall and revenues would fall. But 'willingness-to-pay' studies show that demand is fairly 'inelastic', i.e. non-responsive to price changes, so that by raising prices revenues actually increase. Moreover, demand falls slightly and this is welcome in terms of the carrying capacity of the reserves: many have experienced an excess of tourists with the result that animal behaviour has been changed. The idea of 'optimal' charging for a resource is simple and it allows for ecological considerations to be taken into account as well. The final bonus for the charging policy is that the charging agency, in this case the Kenya Wildlife Service, collects the revenues, reducing its subsidy from the state and giving it potential financial independence.

8.38 A tradeable permit is a permit to emit pollution or to extract a given quantity of a resource (fish, say), but with the important addition that the permit can be bought and sold on the open market. The attraction of this is that those who find pollution control expensive will tend to buy permits and those who find it easier to abate will be willing to sell permits. In this way, pollution control is focused on those who have low costs of abatement, minimising the overall costs of the environmental policy. Moreover, the number of permits issued can be varied. If tighter controls are required, then government can purchase the permits in the open market, lowering the amount of pollution permitted. The effect is then to raise the price of the permits in the open market, stimulating further control by those who now find it cheaper to abate the pollution. As a general rule, abatement will take place whenever the costs of control are less than the price of the permit, and permits will be purchased when the permit price is less than the cost of control. The same principle can be used to ration the use of a resource, and tradeable quotas are quite widely used to control overfishing, forest use, and over-use of water. Congo and Cote d'Ivoire, for example, auction rights to cut forests; Chile and Mexico have systems of tradeable water rights which are issued subject to no infringement of existing rights and subject to ecological low flow constraints. Also in Chile access rights to congested roads are auctioned among taxi and bus operators in an effort to control congestion; and Poland has a pilot emissions trading scheme, as has Almaty in Kazakhstan.

8.39 Clearly, these uses of market based instruments in the developing world are limited, but the fact that they exist at all shows that they have potential and that in any pursuit of sustainable development, they must at least be considered and evaluated. But there is yet another argument that justifies close inspection of market-based instrument systems. Charges, taxes and auctioned permits and quotas all raise revenues. Revenues might be channelled back to the authority which acts as owner of the resource, as with the Kenya Wildlife Service example, or they may accrue to local, regional or central government. The ways in which such revenues are used is important. They might, for example, be used to finance other environmental protection. In short, the potential for environmental taxes and charges is large, and that potential becomes especially important in the context of countries where other measures of taxation may be difficult to implement.

Capturing global values

8.40 Developing countries are often in possession of resources which are highly valued by other countries, or which have a general 'global value'. But markets to capture this global value for the benefit of the countries in question are often absent. There are several ways in which global missing markets can be corrected through creating global environmental markets. It is possible to distinguish between private and public ('official') ventures, and between those that are regulation-induced and those that are spontaneous market initiatives. Public regulation-induced activity arises because of international agreements, such as the Biodiversity and Climate Change Conventions.

8.41 The existence, or threatened existence, of regulations acts as a stimulus to trade. A number of US states and several European countries have policies which limit the amount of carbon dioxide that may be released. These regulations are either self-imposed or reflect obligations under the Framework Convention on Climate Change. Since technologies to control carbon dioxide emissions are very expensive, the kinds of actions needed tend to take the form of energy conservation and fuel switching to low carbon fuels. For some electric utilities, however, even these options may not be available or may be available in only limited form. Such utilities then have an incentive to meet their carbon reduction targets by 'joint implementation' which is enabled, on a pilot basis until the year 2000, under the Climate Convention. The essence of the concept is that country A secures a benefit by reducing emissions or undertaking conservation in country B. A's benefit is the 'credit' under the global environmental agreement, or it may be that A simply seeks a good global 'green image'. Norway has agreed to create additional financing (through the revenues from its own carbon tax) for carbon-reducing projects in Mexico (energy efficient lighting); the US government has a programme of such deals under its Initiative on Joint Implementation which has benefited Central American countries; and in the Netherlands, the state electricity generating board established a non-profit making enterprise in 1990, Forests Absorbing Carbon Dioxide Emissions (FACE), which aims to sequester an amount of carbon dioxide equivalent to that emitted by one 600 MW station (approximately 150,000 hectares of forest, mainly in tropical countries).

8.42 Financial transfers may take place without any regulatory 'push'. The consumer demand for green products has already resulted in companies deciding to invest in conservation either for direct profit or because of a mix of profit and conservation motives. Merck's royalty deal with Costa Rica for pharmaceutical plants is a case in point. The deal between Merck & Co, one of the world's largest pharmaceutical companies, and INBio (the National Biodiversity Institute of Costa Rica) is well documented. Under the agreement, INBio collects and processes plant, insect and soil samples in Costa Rica and supplies them to Merck for assessment. In return, Merck pays Costa Rica US$ one million plus a share of any royalties should any successful drug be developed from the supplied material. The royalty agreement is reputed to be of the order of 1% to 3% and to be shared between INBio and the Costa Rican government. Patent rights to any successful drug would remain with Merck. Biodiversity is protected in two ways – by conferring commercial value on biodiversity, and through the earmarking of some of the payments for the Ministry of Natural Resources.

8.43 A great variety of trades involving both the public and private sectors is possible. For example, consider the general area of resource franchise agreements (RFAs). The general principle of RFAs is that specific land uses in defined zones are restricted ('attenuated') in return for the payment of a premium. The potential buyers could range from local conservation groups through to international conservation societies, corporations, governments and so on, with motives ranging from profiting from sustainable use through to scientific research and good citizenship images.

8.44 Debt-for-Nature Swaps belong to the category of resource franchise agreements. Under such swaps, a body interested in conservation in a given country buys some of the external commercial debt of that country on the open market. Such debt is often 'discounted', i.e. has a market price that is less than 100% of its face value, reflecting the market's assessment of the chances of the debt being repaid. The relevant agency, which could be a conservation body (for example the World

Wide Fund for Nature) then swaps the debt for internal debt, i.e. debt denominated in the domestic currency rather than the foreign currency of the original debt. Effectively, a foreign debt becomes a trust fund or bank account in the indebted country. In return the country agrees to conserve a given environmental asset, often a tropical forest area, but it could be any environmental asset. The indebted country gains from reduced external debt, and may also secure foreign expertise or even clean technology. The conservation agency gains the conservation of a globally valued environmental asset. Domestically, non-government agencies tend to be involved in the management of the conserved asset, raising their status. To date, dozens of such swaps exist and some countries, notably Costa Rica, have retired significant portions of their external debt. Debt reduction is not the main aim of such swaps, but is rather the instrument for securing conservation. Nor would anyone suggest that such swaps should be the main way of retiring debt, but they exemplify the growing number of 'bargains' that generally make all parties better off.

Global environment facility

8.45 The Global Environment Facility (GEF) was created to deal with selected global environmental problems: reduced greenhouse gas emissions, biodiversity conservation, and problems of international shared water resources. It has also taken over the management of the Multilateral Fund that finances the implementation of the Montreal Protocol for the control of ozone depleting substances. Since 1992 it has also been the interim financing mechanism for the Climate Change and Biodiversity Conventions. It is jointly managed by existing UN agencies – United Nations Environmental Programme, the World Bank, and United Nations Development Programme. Its funding (on grant and concessional basis) is intended to be additional to existing sources of aid, and is designed to meet the incremental costs of projects in developing countries which provide global environmental benefits. Following an initial phase, the GEF was restructured and replenished (with US$ 2 billion) in 1994. It is due for further replenishment by the end of 1997.

8.46 An example of a programme the GEF has supported with initial seed-funding of US$ 3 million is the Iwokrama International Rainforest Programme. The Programme arose out of a generous and unprecedented offer by Guyana's government, at the CHOGM in 1989, to set aside almost a million acres of its pristine rain forest for both conservation and sustainable development. A medium-term plan has been drawn up with Commonwealth assistance and additional finance is now being sought to place the Programme on a sound financial footing.

The Iwokrama Programme

The tropical rainforest is a form of ecological capital which provides multiple benefits – economic, environmental and socio-cultural. Can small countries endowed with such forests capture these benefits to meet present needs while conserving the capital for posterity? The Iwokrama Programme, launched with the Commonwealth's blessing and support in 1990, is a practical response to this challenge. Half of the Iwokrama Forest is a Wilderness Preserve where biodiversity is being conserved for scientific research; the remainder will be exploited, in partnership with the private sector, to provide economic benefits on an environmentally sustainable basis. With an agreement signed by the President of Guyana and the Commonwealth Secretary-General at the 1995 CHOGM in New Zealand, legislation was enacted unanimously by Guyana's Parliament in March 1996, guaranteeing the autonomy of the forest area and the Iwokrama International Centre which is responsible for managing it. The Centre has three core programmes: management of the tropical rainforest; conservation and use of biodiversity; and sustainable human development, working in partnership with local Amerindian communities. These are supported by two cross-cutting programmes: research on forests and biodiversity; and information and communication. A donors meeting, co-chaired by the World Bank and the Commonwealth Secretariat and hosted by the European Commission, will be held in October 1997 in order to secure commitments to fund the Centre's basic infrastructure and institutional development. A Consortium is also being formed to enable Commonwealth and non-Commonwealth research institutions with interests in sustainable forest management and biodiversity, to contribute to, as well as benefit from, the Centre's research and training activities.

8.47 The ability of small states to take advantage of arrangements which compensate them for the provision of global environmental benefits, including GEF financing, warrants closer investigation. There are, of course, problems, not least because some feel that bargains of this kind compromise the sovereignty of the developing country. Others would argue that such modification of resource rights is a small price to pay for the economic and environmental benefits that ensue.

Other Innovative Sources of Finance

8.48 Market-based instruments that generate revenues and global value appropriation offer two of the means of financing sustainable development in a world where traditional sources of finance such as foreign aid appear limited. Environmental Funds offer another way of securing finance. These Funds can be generated from revenues obtained from various forms of charges and taxes. In Turkey, for example, a Pollution Prevention Fund is financed from some of the taxes on motor vehicles and from charges for the issue of pollution permits. In Algeria, the National Environmental Fund is financed from charges on airline tickets. In some cases, such as Sri Lanka, Funds have initially been financed by donor contributions. Environmental Funds are not therefore creating something from nothing – a tax or charge base has to exist. But there is evidence that people will more willingly pay a charge if they know that it is being earmarked for an environmental purpose. At the moment, these Funds tend to be marginal in terms of resources raised and expenditures on environmental problems, and they raise the same problems of finding management capacity to handle them. Nonetheless, they are growing in number and extent.

Sectoral Policy

8.49 The previous sections have outlined some of the critical responses that need to be investigated, and where appropriate pursued by small states. Central to policies for sustainable development are domestic reforms on resource and property rights, the correction of price distortions to achieve cost recovery, the implementation of market-based instruments for full cost recovery, proper accounting procedures and economic valuation of environmental assets, and the capture of environmental value through global bargains which reflect the global value of indigenous assets. How do these policy measures translate into sectoral policy? Clearly, measures must be tailored to suit specific issues in specific countries but the 'menu' of measures can best be summarised in a matrix – see Table 8.3. The examples are illustrative only but indicate the wide array of measures that might be adopted to control problems in each sector. As an example, waste management policy can be facilitated by imposing charges on those forms of waste disposal considered to be undesirable because, say, land for landfill is scarce, or because disposal creates a local nuisance. Carefully designed so that other problems do not emerge (e.g. 'flytipping' – illegal landfill), such taxes may yield revenues which can be used to give a subsidy (a credit) to recycling activities. Alternatively, the saved waste disposal costs from recycling can be used to increase the financial return to recycling activity. Liability systems make land users liable for damages e.g. land contamination, whilst land reclamation bonds are taxes on mining and other extractive activities held as bonds and returned to the land owner on successful reclamation of the land at the end of the economic activity. Solid waste disposal is a particularly sensitive issue in many small states which have limited land area or where disposal at sea is not recommended for environmental reasons.

Recommendations

8.50 To reduce environmental vulnerabilities, **small states need to implement strategies which address their most urgent environmental problems and integrate environmental considerations in the earliest stages of economic policy-making.** While their vulnerabilities are shared by many developing countries, they impact on small states in ways which magnify the risk and so require greater and more urgent action than is the case in larger states. Measures to reduce these vulnerabilities also require significantly greater support at regional and international levels.

8.51 At the international level, small states should take a direct interest in promoting the full and effective implementation of a number of environmental conventions and agreements. Among these are the UN Framework Convention on Climate Change; the Convention on Biological Diversity; the Basel Convention on the Control of Transboundary Movements of Hazardous Wastes and Their Safe Disposal; the new International Tropical Timber Agreement and the recommendation of the UN Intergovernmental Panel on Forests; the UN Convention to Combat Desertification; the UN Convention on the Law of the Sea; the UN Agreement on the Conservation and Management of Straddling Fish Stocks and Highly Migratory Fish Stocks; and the 1995 Global Programme of Action for the Protection of the Marine Environment from Land-Based Activities.

Table 8.3 Options for Sectoral Policy

Sector	Issue	Instruments
Macroeconomy	Sustainability	Resource accounting and sustainability indicators Environmentally sensitive economy wide measures
Agriculture	Pollution runoff Soil erosion Pesticide abuse	Remove subsidies Input charges (fertiliser, pesticides) Property rights (soil conservation)
Forestry	Deforestation	Concession bidding Deforestation taxes/royalty taxes Resource franchise agreements (debt for nature, etc.)
Water	Scarcity Pollution Land sterilisation through over-use	Remove subsidies Extraction charges Effluent charges Irrigation charges Tradeable water rights
Solid waste	Local nuisance (odour, vermin) Land scarcity Leachate runoff (landfill) Air pollution (incinerators) Global pollution (landfill-methane; incinerators - CO_2)	Landfill taxes Recycling credits Deposit-refund systems Liability (for hazardous waste)
Wildlife/ecosystem/ tourism	Over-use Pollution	Entry pricing for carrying capacity and revenue maximisation Community incentives Biodiversity prospecting (intellectual property rights) Resource franchising agreements
Seas and coastal zones	Overfishing Coastal pollution Overdevelopment	Tradeable fishing quotas Tradeable development rights

8.52 As the **June 1997 Rio+5 Special Session** of the UN General Assembly in New York clearly revealed, there are serious shortfalls in implementation. The consequences of this are felt in all countries, although small states remain particularly vulnerable. The areas where urgent action needs to be taken in their interest are:

- promoting, in association with Alliance of Small Island States (AOSIS), an effective agreement to reduce greenhouse gas emissions, for adoption by the Conference on Parties to the Convention on Climate Change later this year, as well as assisting the most vulnerable small states to monitor climate change and sea-level rise and protect themselves against their adverse impacts;

- swift ratification and effective implementation of the Convention on Desertification, especially the operation of the Global Mechanism to mobilise funds for its implementation, which has been delayed by disputes over its nature and role;

- support for measures to enhance the management of EEZs, and protect fisheries against illegal fishing by distant water fishing nations, **possibly through a Commonwealth fisheries protection agreement;**

- mobilising support in the international community for full implementation of the Barbados Programme of Action, including accelerating implementation of the Small Island Developing States Information Network (SIDSNET) and Small Island Developing States Technical Assistance Programme (SIDSTAP). **The Commonwealth should play an active role in the 1999 review of the Programme.** The provision of assistance to small states with their technical preparations for the review would also be useful.

8.53 International action is also necessary to mobilise resources to finance sustainable development and compensate for the impacts of natural disasters. The reduction of ODA has been a major constraint in implementing international agreements. This issue dominated the proceedings of the June 1997 Rio+5 UN Special Session. Although the **Global Environment Facility** has emerged as the major multilateral funding mechanism for global environment protection, its resources are modest in relation to needs and its decision-making processes on project approval and disbursements have tended to be complex and cumbersome, inhibiting small states from seeking access to its resources. There is also concern that while the GEF meets the incremental costs of projects in developing countries which help to reduce global warming, there is no comparable mechanism to fund projects (e.g. construction of sea defences) to protect countries from its consequences. It is therefore imperative that:

- the GEF be adequately replenished and further streamlined to improve its operational scope and efficiency;
- the decline in ODA be reversed and that resources be targeted toward supporting environmentally sustainable development.

8.54 There is also a strong case for extending the provision of ODA in the case of **natural disasters**. At present, aid for humanitarian relief is available, but concessional financing to re-build costly infrastructure damaged by natural disasters is much harder to obtain. Small states should seek to establish a natural disasters compensatory financing facility within the UN system which would provide prompt and adequate funds for rehabilitation and reconstruction, bearing in mind both the relatively greater impact that natural disasters have on them and the relatively higher costs of infrastructure than for larger states.

8.55 Small states should also investigate and encourage **innovative approaches to insurance in disaster prone zones**. Neither the use nor the availability of insurance in alleviating the impact of natural disasters is yet satisfactory: individuals residing in hazard-prone areas and commercial insurance companies are reluctant to deal with the problem because of the uncertainty of the risk and the costs incurred. Government insurance funds necessarily tend to be small in smaller countries and vulnerable to single large disaster claims. There is therefore a need to pool national, regional and international resources, both public and private, if comprehensive coverage is to be offered. The Commonwealth Secretariat has investigated the problem and set out a proposal for a multilateral facility which would reinsure catastrophic risks in a central pool. The central pool would be funded by the premiums from the national pools and by some 'seed' money from the UN natural disasters budget. The World Bank's Multilateral Investment Guarantee Agency could take on the task of managing such a facility. This proposal has considerable merit, although it needs further elaboration. Accordingly, we endorse the general thrust behind the proposal and **recommend that urgent consideration be given to the practical problems of implementing such an international insurance system.**

8.56 Small states also need to identify other **innovative forms of finance**. Among those suggested earlier are debt-for-nature swaps; developing partnerships with the private sector to exploit biodiversity and share equitably in the consequent benefits; resource franchise agreements; and the establishment of environmental trust funds. There is considerable scope for such measures in conserving biodiversity and coral reefs, managing forests sustainably, and improving fisheries management. Others include measures which market products which conform to sustainable development practices, as proposed in the case of bananas from the Eastern Caribbean. **Small states should be given appropriate international and regional assistance in identifying such sources of finance** and, as crucially, technical support in negotiating such agreements with the private sector, NGOs and donor agencies.

8.57 Evidence is mounting that **market-based economic instruments** are often a more cost-effective way of achieving environmental goals than are traditional 'command and control' regulatory approaches. This involves the removal of government subsidies, which encourage high-pollution and over-exploitation of resources by lowering the 'price' of pollution and resource consumption; and the proper pricing of goods and services to reflect their 'true' environmental costs, thereby creating the incentives for resources to be used in an environmentally sustainable manner. Among the sectors in small states where such approaches would yield immediate benefit are tourism (entry charges to terrestrial and marine national parks and diving fees for access to coral reefs); efficient energy pricing and the removal of subsidies which encourage profligate energy consumption; pricing water as an economic good at a level which reflects its scarcity and environmental cost, with due regard to the need to satisfy basic human needs for adequate and safe water; and the use of tradeable fishing quotas, where appropriate, to control fishing. Small states should consider adopting these measures as a matter of priority.

8.58 This will require action by governments both to **incorporate environmental thinking into macroeconomic management** and to strengthen capacity in policy formation and implementation. The former requires proper valuation of the environment through measures such as 'green national accounting'. The latter requires improving or establishing co-ordination within and between national agencies responsible for development planning, natural resource management and environmental monitoring and protection. Other priorities include strengthening capacities:

• for biodiversity monitoring and assessment, particularly in some small islands where species endemism is very high but the capacity for biodiversity conservation is limited;

• for sustainable forest management and its financing in countries which face institutional, human and other resource constraints;

- for monitoring water quality and increasing investment in projects designed to increase access to safe water and sanitation;

- in countries which suffer from desertification and drought, to promote environmentally sustainable agriculture and implement comprehensive rural development policies;

- to improve the surveillance and monitoring of EEZs;

- to improve the implementation of effective coastal zone management policies.

In many of these areas regional co-operation would provide significant additional inputs to improving national capacity.

8.59 Finally, we welcome major environmental initiatives of global significance taken by small states. A prominent example is the **Iwokrama International Rainforest Programme** in Guyana. The programme is unique in attempting to demonstrate that the tropical rainforest can be so managed that environmental and economic goals can be pursued in harmony and mutual support. It can become a model for best practice with benefits flowing to Guyana, the rest of the Commonwealth and the global community. **We urge Commonwealth and non-Commonwealth donors to provide the support which the Programme now needs** in order to become financially viable and fulfill its mission.

9

The Political Dimension: Analysis

9.1 The vulnerability of small states to threats depends to a considerable extent on the security environment in which they are located. Since all are classified as developing countries they will face security problems which are similar to other developing countries but qualitatively different from more developed countries. As small states they are also particularly sensitive to geopolitical realities which in turn underlines the need to take into account the regional context. The 1985 *Vulnerability* report identified the Caribbean, the South Pacific, the Indian Ocean and Africa as distinct regions with their own security problems. These remain valid categories and the development of regionalism in the post-Cold War period suggests that greater emphasis than before needs to be placed on the region as well as recognising important sub-regional variations. What follows is an overview of the major security challenges which have arisen since the survey in the *Vulnerability* report, identifying the important political dimensions of economic and environmental threats as well as more specific military and political concerns.

The Caribbean

9.2 The Caribbean continues to be faced with demanding security problems. There was a major incident in Trinidad and Tobago in 1990 when members of a fundamentalist sect took the Prime Minister and seven of his ministers hostage. The situation was quickly brought to an end with no major loss of life. The circumstances of the coup, however, were a textbook demonstration of how comparatively few men with guns can seriously compromise the security of a small state. This was an isolated, country specific incident and there has not been any fallout effect in the rest of the region. It should be noted, however, that both in Trinidad and Tobago, as in the Maldives, the logistics for holding a trial of the coup leaders placed quite a strain on the administrative and security resources of a small state, and in the former case, the costs of holding the subsequent trials turned out to be considerable.

9.3 It is the activities of non-state actors which currently are the source of greatest concern in the region. Its position as a chain of small units linking North and South America makes the Caribbean a perfect communications link, and this has been exploited by criminal elements engaged in the trade of high value illegal goods and services, mainly connected with drugs. The region, from Belize to Guyana, is a principal transit area for both American and European destinations with as much as 40% of the yearly import of cocaine in the US said to pass through the Caribbean. Illegal trafficking in drugs is controlled by national and international cartels, using state-of-the-art communications systems and possessing effective coercive capability for enforcement of their will within communities and, if necessary, willingness to use force against state security. All countries are at risk but in the last decade those that have been the most targeted include The Bahamas, Belize, Guyana, Jamaica and Trinidad and Tobago. The Eastern Caribbean has also been ensnared, particularly in trafficking drugs to EU countries.

9.4 Drug trafficking has also directly threatened the social fabric of the concerned small states, as it has stimulated both increased drug production and consumption in the region, apart from fostering corruption and feeding other criminal elements. Indeed, some regional analysts consider the activities of international criminal elements to be the most serious threat facing the region now, and over the next few decades. Since the US is the major destination for the drugs, that country's 'war on drugs' has inevitably meant that these small states are drawn into both co-operation and conflict scenarios with their superpower neighbour. Among the most controversial have been ship-rider arrangements which place Caribbean personnel aboard US coast guard ships, thereby providing a basis for the US to board vessels, arrest suspects and confiscate drugs in the territorial waters of Caribbean states. States permitting this include Antigua and Barbuda, Belize, Dominica, Grenada, Guyana, St Kitts and Nevis, St Lucia, St Vincent and the Grenadines, and Trinidad and Tobago. Barbados and Jamaica have now also concluded agreements which meet their concerns about the preservation of their national sovereignty.

9.5 An allied problem is money laundering. The Caribbean is the site of the greatest concentration of offshore financial centres in the developing world. The growth of these in the 1980s and into the 1990s has been linked to the transnationalisation of finance and investment. They provide services for which there is a rising legitimate demand and which are functional to the development of international capital. At the same time the conditions of confidentiality and permissive legal frameworks that surround their activities offer facilities that are useful to the criminal and the drug trafficker. Much of the concern has centred on banks and businesses established in the British dependent territories and in the Netherlands Antilles, but as other independent countries have joined The Bahamas in offering such services the need to develop a vigorous policy to combat money laundering has gathered momentum. Of note here have been actions taken by the Caribbean Financial

Action Task Force and by the Commonwealth Secretariat. Any effective programme against money laundering should take into account that the problems for small states occur both at the time of of the enactment of legislation and regulatory regimes and later at the enforcement stage.

9.6 Regional security effectiveness was enhanced when Belize and Guyana were able to overcome the barrier to their membership of the Organisation of American States (OAS) which had existed because of their territorial disputes with OAS member states, Guatemala and Venezuela respectively. This success owed much to co-ordinated and sustained regional pressure by the CARICOM member states of the OAS which made the issue one of their priority concerns in that organisation. Progress was also made on several territorial issues. The maritime dispute between Venezuela and Trinidad and Tobago was eventually settled by a treaty in 1990. Although the Venezuela–Guyana issue has been the subject of some political accommodation over the last decade it has not receded as a major political issue. Suriname also has a territorial claim against Guyana. While Guatemala has not formally abandoned its claim, in 1991 it made substantial concessions and deflated the issue considerably by, for the first time, recognising the sovereignty of Belize and establishing diplomatic relations. Against this background there have been ongoing consultations between Belize and Guatemala on the implementation of confidence-building measures. There has been no need for several years to convene the Commonwealth Ministerial Committee on Belize but the discussion of the issue at each Commonwealth summit is a useful way to indicate that Commonwealth monitoring continues.

9.7 Although the regional small states have good relations with Cuba, they have to deal with the reality that, for the US, Cuba remains an unsettled Cold War issue, and that this could have unwelcome repercussions for them. An example is the 'The Cuban Liberty and Democratic Solidarity (Libertad) Act', popularly known as the Helms-Burton Act. This allows US citizens to seek compensation in the US courts against third parties 'trafficking' in properties 'confiscated' from them by the Cuban government and allows the US government to suspend US visas granted to foreign nationals who have 'benefited' from or 'trafficked' in such properties. The extraterritorial reach of the legislation has been condemned by CARICOM and by the OAS, among others, and while there has been some immediate mitigation of its application, its long-term effect can only be discouraging to CARICOM's attempts to 'normalise' relations with Cuba.

9.8 Refugees and illegal migrants continue to be a major problem in the cases of Haitians and Cubans into The Bahamas and Guatemalans into Belize, not only at the political level, but as a considerable strain in administrative and financial terms. Over the years The Bahamas has developed a sophisticated policy of accommodation that is a credit to a small state. Belize also has adjusted well, but its problem is more complex, given the territorial claim of Guatemala. Because of the small population of the receiving states the number of permanent settlers who have entered over the last few decades are a significant addition.

9.9 Another source of unwelcome migrants, and one which has very destabilising effects in a small state, comes from the developing custom in certain metropolitan states of systematic deportation to the region of significant numbers of drug-related and other violent criminals who are Caribbean nationals. The effect has been to deepen the sophistication of criminal activity in concerned countries and territories, with the local police often being at a disadvantage in terms of the weapons used. A regional source has commented, 'they leave our islands as high school criminals and return to us as postgraduates'. The US is also a significant source of firearms which are illegally diverted to other countries.

9.10 Thus both with drugs and refugees, two cases where the destination which generates the market is the regional great power, that power seeks to use offshore small states as a buffer in managing the problem, adding unnecessary and expensive burdens to these societies. Jamaican officials, for example, have estimated that security measures by the garment industry to combat drug smuggling add 8% to operating costs. They have also been the major recipient of deported criminals.

9.11 The Caribbean has also been involved in a considerable effort to deal with the problem of the transit of hazardous and radioactive waste. The region has one of the highest densities of cruise liners and of cargo vessels (including many tankers) in the world with a commensurably higher risk of pollution. It has also been concerned with the shipment of spent nuclear fuel (plutonium) from Japanese nuclear reactors through the region, with at least six such shipments between 1992 and 1996. In 1995, CARICOM Heads of Government issued an important Statement which addressed their concern about the matter.

9.12 Where small states abut a very large, powerful, energetic neighbour, the spill over effects of its policies in areas such as drugs, general crime, pollution and the spread of corruption can have devastating effects on fragile societies unless that power is sensitive and benign. It also has to be aware of the wider impact of policies. One particularly telling example is in relation to the banana industry. The Caribbean depends on guaranteed access to the EU market to maintain its exports. This is done under the banana regime of the EU which has been the product of difficult and protracted negotiations in the EU and with the US and Latin American producers. The decision by the US and several Latin American countries to challenge its legality in the WTO, and the recent finding by the WTO's Dispute Settlement Body which calls for changes to the regime, is a body-blow to several countries in the Eastern Caribbean. There is no ready alternative to the employment and foreign exchange the industry generates. If it is allowed to collapse the effects, in the words of one report, will be 'disastrous' with 'severe economic consequences' contributing to 'socially unmanageable fallout' and an 'explosive political situation'.

9.13 Finally, and although low key, the possibility of secession is always present. The announcement by the Premier of Nevis that steps would be taken to separate from St Kitts occasioned early action by the Chairman of CARICOM and an offer by the Commonwealth to seek to resolve differences.

The South Pacific

9.14 Over the last decade the security challenges in the South Pacific have been a mixture of conventional issues and environmental ones. Fiji and Papua New Guinea are the only two states with significant military establishments and it is these two states which have had major security problems. The former was the only case of a successful takeover of a government by military coup in the region in contemporary times and it is a mark of its political unacceptability that, many years later, Fiji remains estranged from the Commonwealth. Much depends on the outcome of the constitutional review process which began in 1993.

9.15 Papua New Guinea has a long permeable border with Indonesia, but its neighbour is so large and has such a sophisticated military capacity that Papua New Guinea prefers to approach its border problems at the diplomatic level. However, over the long term, this border is likely to remain a potential security problem.

9.16 Papua New Guinea has also had to deal with a unique challenge to its territorial integrity – the attempted breakaway of Bougainville. The first attempt at secession in 1975/76 was non-violent and ended in a constitutional solution. The second, begun in 1989, has been marked by violence with direct casualties from the conflict numbering in the hundreds and direct and indirect costs running into billions of dollars. The success of the rebels of the Bougainville Revolutionary Army in establishing control over the copper mine (which closed) was facilitated by the inexperience of a small state army and the clearly indicated regional disapproval of an all-out war.

9.17 In late 1994 a ceasefire was brokered and negotiations began, but broke down in early 1996 with the resumption of violence. The recruitment of mercenaries led to difficulties between the government and the Papua New Guinea Defence Force. While the involvement of mercenaries has been condemned internationally it is also striking that even though the rebellion has lasted eight years, no regional state has recognised the rebels. By and large, the spill over into the Solomon Islands excepted, the matter has been seen as one internal to Papua New Guinea, with the most significant regional involvement to date being the establishment of a South Pacific Regional Peacekeeping Force which was sent to Bougainville in October 1994 as part of the process of negotiation. The Bougainville issue is clearly problematic, but to many observers it is also manageable and does not represent any developing regional trend.

9.18 The continuing colonial issue of the political evolution of the French territory of New Caledonia has long been a matter of concern in the region. In the 1980s the Melanesian states of Papua New Guinea, Vanuatu and Solomon Islands created the Melanesian Spearhead Group to support the independence campaign in international fora. The 1980s were also marked by several outbreaks of major violence as it became clear that France was not about to grant independence readily in the face of the opposition of the territory's powerful European population. The small states of the region have always looked upon the issue as having the potential for creating international tensions and disrupting regional security; thus through their regional organisation, the South Pacific Forum, they have pursued a resolution of the matter directly with the French and, in particular, at the UN, including mobilising support in the Asian region.

9.19 New Caledonia is now becoming a pressing matter as the ten year moratorium on the issue of political independence agreed in the Matignon Accords of 1988 is coming to an end. The intervening period has been marked by an absence of political violence, but the underlying causes of earlier disruption remain and may have become exacerbated by the further concentration of economic wealth in the hands of the Europeans at the relative expense of the rest of the population. The referendum on the status of New Caledonia is due in 1998. In the past, elections have been associated with violence and this cannot be ruled out in the future, particularly as the result is likely to be contentious. It may also have ripple effects elsewhere with elements in French Polynesia building on gathering support for independence in their territory.

9.20 A principal area of concern is environmental issues, in particular the use of the Pacific Ocean and some islands for the dumping of nuclear waste and for nuclear testing. A remark by the President of the Marshall Islands that his government was considering the possibility of establishing an international facility for destroying and disposing of nuclear waste on islands already contaminated by nuclear testing became a matter of concern at a SPF meeting in 1994. Several years earlier island governments had expressed concern over US plans to destroy chemical weapons on Johnston Atoll. In 1995 the SPF adopted the Waigani Convention which banned the importation of all hazardous and radioactive waste into Forum island countries and sought to ensure that any transboundary movement of hazardous waste within the area was controlled in an environmentally sound manner. It also reiterated its opposition to dumping of radioactive waste at sea and expressed its belief that the chemical weapons destruction facility at Johnston Atoll should be closed when the current programme was completed.

9.21 In the early 1990s there was increased concerted regional opposition to French nuclear testing, and a mobilisation of international opinion led by the SPF. The success of these efforts owed much to France's international isolation on this matter and to the timing, but it also was a demonstration both of effective protest tactics and of a sustained diplomatic initiative by a grouping of small states. As part of that campaign the regional states in 1985 agreed on the Treaty of Rarotonga declaring the area the South Pacific Nuclear Free Zone. It prohibits the manufacture, stationing or testing of any nuclear explosive device in the treaty area and includes Protocols seeking to limit the nuclear powers from testing in the region. All five nuclear states have now undertaken to respect its provisions and so far four, the former Soviet Union in 1986 and France, the UK and the USA in 1996, have signed the Protocols to the treaty. The SPF has always held a strong position on nuclear issue and those issues tend to loom large at their annual meetings. The Forum suspended France's status as a 'Dialogue Partner' (and thus her right to participate in the post-Forum consultative meetings) during the dispute over the resumption of testing in September 1995 but agreed to its return at the 1996 Forum. The resolute opposition by the SPF (as a crucial element of world-wide opposition to the testing) is held by many to have prompted France to call off the tests early.

The Indian Ocean

9.22 Because of the vast gaps between them in the immense reaches of the Indian Ocean, the small states of that region, Mauritius, the Seychelles and the Maldives do not interact in a functional subregional political or security agency. Mauritius and Seychelles have not had any significant security challenges over the past decade. By contrast in 1988 externally located dissidents, nationals of the Maldives, attempted to take over the government in an invasion by sea and involving the use of foreign mercenaries. India rapidly and successfully, came to the aid of the Maldives and the attackers were captured. The Maldives and the international community welcomed and praised the Indian contribution as a timely and merited neighbourly exercise.

9.23 After the coup the Maldives sought to mobilise international opinion on the issue of the protection of small states by successfully piloting through the UN in 1989, a resolution calling on that body to examine the matter (GARes.44/51). However, in the Security Council discussion, there was no agreement as to whether small states deserved a special security status and the issue foundered especially as the number of returns from member states to the Secretary General's invitation to submit suggestions on the issue were very low. The adoption of the International Convention Against the Recruitment, Use, Financing and Training of Mercenaries by the UN General Assembly is of great relevance to countries like the Seychelles, Maldives and Papua New Guinea.

9.24 A low level but persistent problem is raised by the US military facilities on Diego Garcia. Originally the islands were administered from Mauritius but were detached from it immediately prior to independence to form the British Indian Ocean Territory. They were then leased to the US by the UK. Currently both Mauritius and the UK claim sovereignty. Mauritius is unlikely to seek a resolution of the issue in the immediate future although the potential for it to become one remains and may be precipitated by use of the base to project military power (as recently in Operation Desert Storm) or by any decision of the US to withdraw before its lease expires in 2025.

9.25 Other security concerns with a pronounced political dimension have included the subtle influence of France in the South-West Indian Ocean and the potential spill-over of rivalries among countries of the littoral leading to an increased military presence in the region. There may be problems of boundary delimitation if offshore petroleum is discovered or over fisheries rights. The Indian Ocean remains an important strategic region because of the Gulf oil shipping lanes. The most important threats, however, remain internally generated.

The Mediterranean

9.26 Cyprus, though not typical of small state security issues, continues to be a seemingly intractable security problem. Since the invasion and occupation by Turkey of the northern part of the island in 1974, there have been a number of attempts by the UN, including one currently underway, to find a solution but all have so far failed to make substantial progress. Among the objectives for a solution, as set out in UN resolutions and endorsed by the Commonwealth, are the speedy withdrawal of Turkish forces and settlers, the return of refugees to their homes in safety, the restoration and respect of human rights of all Cypriots, and accounting for missing persons. There has also been considerable concern over the increasing number of Turkish settlers and the level of forces. Turkey keeps a large military force of some 35,000 on the island. Recent proposals by the Cypriot government for the complete demilitarisation of the Republic of Cyprus have been welcomed by the international community and supported by the Commonwealth.

9.27 UN policy as expressed in numerous resolutions, in addition to the objectives cited above, favours a settlement based on a bi-communal, bi-zonal federation with a constitution approved by both the Greek-Cypriot and Turkish-Cypriot communities, with effective participation of both communities in a federal government. The Commonwealth, recognising that the issue has been a dispute primarily within the jurisdiction of the Security Council, continues to support the UN's role in reaching a settlement. The Commonwealth Action Group on Cyprus, created by the 1975 CHOGM, continues to monitor developments and facilitate the UN Secretary-General's efforts and to support the independence, sovereignty, territorial integrity and unity of the Republic of Cyprus. These goals have been reaffirmed by the Commonwealth Heads of Government in their meetings over the years since 1974, including the most recent meeting in Auckland.

9.28 Malta has not had a significant security threat in recent years. Its status of neutrality as well as the end of the Cold War have made it less vulnerable to military threats. It is now developing into an important centre for regional co-operation. However, Malta's openness has created new threats in the form of money laundering and of drug trafficking, smuggling contraband goods and illegal migration through Malta into Europe.

Africa

9.29 Before the removal of the apartheid regime, South Africa pursued a policy of intimidating and destabilising its neighbours, including the small states of Botswana, Lesotho and Swaziland, on whom the impact was greater because of the political, economic and strategic stranglehold in which Pretoria held these states. When it chose, it would intervene through direct military incursion, quite apart from a range of subversive techniques. That era is over, but while post-apartheid South Africa is a friendly regional partner, it remains the leading regional power whose internal stability and external policies necessarily impact on the neighbouring small states including those in the Indian Ocean.

9.30 The Gambia has, by contrast, been free of any serious threat from its neighbours. In 1982 it entered into a confederal arrangement with Senegal which was dissolved in 1989. The impetus behind confederation were security concerns in The Gambia and Senegal's fear of instability in The Gambia which, from time to time, has led it to commit military forces in support of the Gambian government. The most recent manifestation of instability was in July 1994 when the army overthrew the government in a bloodless military coup. Since then The Gambia has come under considerable external pressure to restore democracy. Elections returning the government to civilian rule were finally held, though under controversial conditions, in 1997. The Commonwealth played a major role in monitoring the return to civilian democratic rule in The Gambia through the mechanism of the Commonwealth Ministerial Action Group on the Harare Declaration and through providing technical assistance.

9.31 Lesotho has also been troubled by regime instability and military coup. Civilian government was restored after seven years of military rule in 1993. However, tensions between it, the armed forces and the King remained high and led to the dismissal of the government by the King in August 1994. This triggered intervention by Botswana, South Africa and Zimbabwe to restore the government and subsequently the King abdicated in favour of his father. The Commonwealth has also played advisory and active good offices roles in these developments.

9.32 Swaziland has also experienced some political unrest in recent years. This has been the consequence of power struggles in the ruling monarchy and of attempts at political reform. In 1993, elections were held, but a ban on political parties was in force at the time which has led some observers to question their fairness. There were also violent trade union-led protests in 1995.

9.33 All the African countries have had problems with refugees and/or with borders. The end of the wars in Mozambique and Angola, along with the end of apartheid, have considerably diminished the problem in South Africa. With the exception of a minor border dispute between Namibia and Botswana, which has been referred to the International Court of Justice for adjudication, there are no contentious issues at present.

Assessment

9.34 What is striking about the overview is the diversity of threats which have faced the various regions. While some identified in the *Vulnerability* report have dropped out (ideological rivalry in the Caribbean and the Indian Ocean, plus the end of the apartheid regime in South Africa) others have proved remarkably durable (environmental and decolonisation concerns in the South Pacific) while others (notably the occupation and division of Cyprus) are seemingly as intractable as ever and the cause of Commonwealth and international concern. Additionally, while there have been coups or attempted coups as well as significant regime instability in four of the regions (Caribbean, South Pacific, Indian Ocean and Africa) the outstanding characteristic has been the specificity of each case, underlining both the fact of general vulnerability and individual circumstance. An individual security audit therefore remains necessary to comprehend the particular configuration of political threats facing any small state as at the same time it is evident that many small states share similar if not identical security profiles.

9.35 It therefore still remains possible to identify a small state security problem in a political and military sense. This derives in large part from weakness in relation to other powers and instability in its social and political institutions. The former appears to be of less relevance than it was a decade ago. Small states then had to be mindful of the interests of superpowers and while they still need to be aware of great power manipulation it has been largely absent from the threats identified above. Small states have also not become the deliberate targets of revisionist states or of regional hegemons. This is not to argue that they will not have to confront such threats in the less structured international system which has emerged from the Cold War, but for the moment they are potential rather than actual threats. The most pressing threats small states face in the international system have been from the growth of transnational activity which has multiplied the number of non-state actors, some of whom are criminal in activity and intent.

9.36 International criminal elements have taken advantage of communications advances to network their activities on a world-wide scale and made serious incursions into small states which, initially, were practically without, and continue for the most part to lack, relevant defence against this type of criminal activity. The need for enhanced international assistance in this area cannot be overemphasised, and is well merited as clearly these small states are very much pawns in an international game.

9.37 With great power budgetary constraints and a reduction in their naval global presence, there is the danger that criminal elements may feel freer to engage in a range of illegal activities, including piracy, on the high seas. Such piracy is likely to grow considerably over the next few decades – and in sophisticated forms. Multi-island states may be very vulnerable to their activities and to their need for havens.

9.38 The awareness of the dangers of international crime has been improving as the international community may be gradually coming to appreciate that, in the case of narcotics, this is a global issue which needs to be fought with global resources and co-ordination. For small states a particular problem is at the domestic level, where a great increase in the use of drugs is often a fallout from the country being used by the international drugs mafia as a conduit for the international drug trade. The impact in a small society of a mushrooming drug problem is comprehensively devastating.

9.39 Over the last decade a significant increase in domestic crime is emerging in some states as a dangerous social and physical threat since their small scale and open, relaxed societies makes them vulnerable to being easily terrorised. This is especially so because of the state-of-the-art weaponry and communications systems which the criminals often possess and which usually are superior to those of the local police. The international community needs to accept that the continual development of sophisticated weaponry and communications creates ready victims in some parts of the globe, and to consider what is the global responsibility for law and order at this level.

9.40 The other threat is political and social instability. The majority of security threats which arose in the last two decades have been domestic in source; that is, they were regime threats rather than state threats since the state itself has hardly been threatened save in the few secession cases. The major sources of discontent in 'developing states' are economic hardships, questions of political legitimacy, authoritarian rule, ethnic violence and military dissension. Small states have experienced all of these, but the indications are that, outside of cases of ethnic violence, the moderating of economic hardships is the key variable. In geopolitical terms there are, in Commonwealth small states, very few cases where ethnic violence can possibly lead directly to interstate conflict. Cyprus is the obvious exception. Elsewhere, there are, at present, no significant ethnic issues, in terms of potential for violent conflict, simmering below the surface, but there are situations which, in the absence of sensitive, participatory and fair dealings, can get out of hand given the geographically small areas of some of these states and/or the residential juxtaposition of some nationalities.

9.41 But, in general, it is fair to conclude that in comparison to larger states, small states exhibit an enviable record of political stability. The incidence of civil disorder is low; social pressures to conform are high; and political preference for maintenance of the status quo is higher still. Nevertheless, political order does, on occasion, break down and when it occurs the effect is always magnified, precisely because the political and social system is small. Personal, familial, group and community relations are strained weakening social ties and politicising them. International events and issues can become domestic flash-points and domestic tensions and rivalries become internationalised with little or no warning. Small states can be traumatised when conflicts intensify. There is therefore no room for complacency since the stakes can very quickly escalate beyond the survival of a particular regime to the survival of the core values of the society itself.

10

The Political Dimension: Response and Recommendations

10.1 In the 1985 *Vulnerability* report a range of measures were suggested to reduce vulnerability which continue to be relevant since they were based on an analysis of the basic character and condition of small states. The recommendations stressed the development of skills, the need for an unremitting diplomatic effort, maintaining and strengthening democracy, varied and relevant security provisions, appropriate regional institutions and sustained and adequate international financial and technical assistance over a wide range of areas. While many states have taken steps to implement the recommendations at the national and/or regional levels, the efforts have been limited more because of lack of financial and technical resources than because of lack of will. In the wake of the Grenada crisis and the *Vulnerability* report there was some donor interest but that has not been sustained, especially as there was no evidence of a significant threat pattern in conventional terms. Each seemed to be *sui generis*, were usually dramatic acts of discontent rather than revolutions and were not repeating themselves.

10.2 Small states have therefore had to take or maintain the initiative in developing security policies for themselves. This chapter will examine the measures open to enhance the political security of small states at national, bilateral and regional levels where small states can expect to define agendas and policies particularly suited to their needs.

The National Level

10.3 Small state security starts at home. It has a number of dimensions but three in particular stand out. The deployment of sufficient enforcement capabilities to anticipate and manage internal threats to the state and to meet minor external aggression; the maintenance of social integrity; and most importantly the development of policy capacity.

Enforcement capabilities

10.4 There are 20 Commonwealth small states with professional military forces: Antigua and Barbuda, The Bahamas, Barbados, Belize, Botswana, Brunei Darussalam, Cyprus, The Gambia, Guyana, Jamaica, Lesotho, Maldives, Malta, Mauritius, Namibia, Papua New

Guinea, Seychelles, Swaziland, Trinidad and Tobago, and Tonga. All small states have police forces and intelligence capacity and most have developed para-military capabilities and in the case of island states, coastguard provision. Few countries have a significant air wing.

10.5 The level of armed forces per capita and their configuration varies from state to state but the one common denominator is that all lack the capability to mount sustained or major unilateral operations beyond their home state. The armed forces are therefore oriented to internal security. Even here they can be seriously constrained in action against determined resistance or prove to be inadequate against a major external intervention, as the case of Cyprus demonstrates. In such circumstances the recruitment of external forces is a temptation. The intended use of mercenaries in Bougainville was a case in point and also an example of the perils that can attach to such action. This, of course, is not to be confused with legally sanctioned stationing of armed forces who may, as in the case of the Gurkha forces in Brunei, be primarily of foreign origin.

10.6 Where professional armed forces do not exist police forces have in many instances acquired para-military capabilities. This is the case in the Eastern Caribbean and for Vanuatu and the Solomon Islands. Coastguards may also be separately established or be part of the armed forces or the police. The value of an effective coastguard has come to be recognised more and more in recent years and despite its cost there has been a relative expansion of this provision in the small island states. International efforts to develop the national capacities of small states in the surveillance and monitoring of the coasts and EEZs as well as the high seas are being undertaken on a regional basis. In the smallest states internal security is provided by police forces.

10.7 There have been significant efforts to improve information and intelligence networks and to upgrade and diversify the defence estab-lishment. Intelligence has become especially important as criminal activity has internationalised. Nevertheless there has not generally been any significant increase in defence forces or defence budgets or any substantial aid grants for the upgrading of their equipment or technical competence. Objectively, however, the states are exceptionally vulnerable, and there is a need to bolster the provisions for enhancing their conventional security as the potential for new insecurity scenarios is high in the more open post-Cold War arena where the focus of attention is on other, more pressing, theatres.

Social integrity

10.8 The social cohesion of small states is essential whether the country is socio-culturally homogeneous or plural. It is not simply a matter of ethnicity – although this constitutes the most divisive and potentially most destabilising cleavage in some small states – but is also a question of groups who may be disadvantaged or feel themselves to be so. These include fundamentalist sects and immigrants as well as broader categories such as women and youth.

10.9 The growth of fundamentalism in recent years is a matter of concern to many small states, particularly as it is clear that in the past fundamentalist movements have been linked to mass suicide, secession and to coup attempts. There is no easy answer to this question. While it may be monitored via intelligence, it has to be accommodated or countered in a wider social context in which the aims and values of the country are known and shared by the majority.

10.10 Small states are hosts to long-stay visitors and immigrants as well as providers of emigrants. The attractions can be climate as in the case of retirees and higher income earners in the Caribbean and the South Pacific or economic opportunity provided by tourism and relatively higher standards of living compared to their own developing countries as in the Indian Ocean and the African states. It can also be a matter of geography as in infiltration over porous borders in enclave states or islands in the path of a refugee exodus. In the face of such population movements most small states have been tolerant and even welcoming when incomers bring scarce skills and financial resources. Economic citizenship programmes are being promulgated by many small states as a means of securing much-needed scarce foreign exchange earnings as well as attracting investment. But small states will also need to be increasingly aware of pressures on the carrying capacity of the state and in the case of islands on the erosion of cultural distinctiveness. National policies to address these issues may be needed sooner rather than later and in the case of citizenship programmes policies for control and monitoring of abuses by holders of such citizenships should be strengthened.

10.11 It is not at all clear whether women or youth suffer any greater disadvantage in small states than in larger ones. In the case of women it might be inferred that because small states tend to be conservative and traditionalist women will not be treated equally with men. At the same time women have reached high office in some small states and in the Caribbean they currently have a higher proportion successfully completing higher education than do men. In the case of youth there is again a better record of achievement in education in smaller states than in larger ones, although this is offset by more limited employment opportunities and a corresponding interest and desire for emigration. In both cases the real questions are equalities of opportunity in education and employment as well as the wider issue of social justice. Women of whatever age and in all societies need to be secure from personal violence and be empowered to take control over the key decisions affecting their lives. Likewise youth need encouragement and instruction, not least in good citizenship where through cross-cultural, cross-racial and cross-religious group projects in the fields of social welfare, education and recreation they can provide the cement of national integration.

Policy capacity

10.12 The promotion of representative and responsive government is vital to the security of small states. Without it there will be discontent, distress, disorder and potentially disaster if the state implodes or becomes subject to hostile intervention. To guard against such calamities small states need to develop a consensual, adaptive and effective policy capacity. This demands more than the creation of a coherent and efficient executive and administration – important as these are. It also requires a large measure of agreement about the ends and means of security, which requires, in turn, legitimacy and openness in the political system and the ability to combine defence, foreign and domestic policies into one integrated security policy.

10.13 Legitimacy and openness are best served where popular participation in politics, including the opportunity openly to dissent, is assured and when the basic rights of citizens, including entrenched provision for the protection of minority groups, are widely respected and guaranteed by law. In a word, when good governance prevails. This is now widely understood and is a central feature of membership of the Commonwealth as set out in the Harare Declaration of 1991 and reaffirmed in the Millbrook Commonwealth Action Programme on the Harare Declaration in 1995. Fortunately, small states meet most of the criteria for good governance most of the time. Those that do not, as well as some that do but have felt the need for wider approbation, have taken significant steps in this direction in recent years. Among recent instances that may be cited where the Commonwealth has played a crucial role are the observation of elections in the Seychelles in 1992 and 1993 which marked a transition from a one-party to a multi-party system of government; the Lesotho elections in 1993 which saw a change from military rule to multi-party democracy; elections in Namibia in 1994 which consolidated the democratic process in the country; and in St Kitts and Nevis in 1995 which confirmed long established democratic practice. On the other hand Presidential elections held in The Gambia in 1996 have been criticised, leading to freer Parliamentary elections in 1997. Other recent assistance has included the Secretary-General's 'good offices' in resolving tensions between the armed forces and the government and the armed forces and the police in Lesotho and a similar 'good offices' role played by the Secretary-General in Papua New Guinea in early 1997. Offers of 'good offices' and technical assistance have also been made in Swaziland in the area of constitutional review.

10.14 The need for an integrated security policy at national level not only arises from the need for a multidimensional approach but also from the need to broaden the security debate in small states. All too often the security of such states is the responsibility of only a few individuals who meet infrequently and respond only to the immediate issues in front of them. A wider vision is lacking. Yet, it should be apparent that such a vision, emanating from publicly accountable mechanisms through which threats and vulnerabilities are perceived and assessed, resources are allocated, and policies are selected and implemented, constitutes an indispensable basis for a credible and shared national security policy which will uphold public order and meet external threat. The need for secrecy on intelligence matters and even force levels in the smallest states is understood, but this needs to be traded off against a consensus on security in government and opposition which only a bipartisan approach to security will guarantee. More generally, such an approach, when widened to incorporate expert advice from a range of senior administrators across a gamut of government services, will not only ensure all eventualities are foreseen as far as possible but as importantly enjoy public confidence, which in itself is of inestimable value in providing the bedrock of security in small states.

Bilateral Arrangements

10.15 The security of many small states has in the past been enhanced by a variety of formal arrangements or informal 'understandings' between small states and regional or great powers that the latter will come to their support in times of distress or acute need. This has been the case in the Caribbean, the South Pacific, the Indian Ocean and should have been the case in Cyprus under the Treaty of Guarantee which formed part of the independence arrangements for the island in 1960 but which proved counterproductive and ineffective in 1974. The countries which small states have looked to to provide such support have been the United States, Britain and Canada in the Caribbean; the United States, Australia and New Zealand in the South Pacific; and India in the case of the Maldives.

10.16 The involvement of the United States has at times been contentious, especially in the Caribbean. Relations with Britain and Canada have been good and their involvement has been welcomed.

British armed forces were stationed in Belize under a special under-standing which strengthened Belizian security in the face of Guatemalan claims on its territory and Britain and Canada have provided support for the regional security system in the Eastern Caribbean as well as to individual Caribbean states.

10.17 The security 'understanding' between the small states in the South Pacific and Australia and New Zealand is often held up as a 'model' form of association. It is not without its critics, but on the whole evaluations are positive and tensions in relationships are less acute than for US relations in the Caribbean. Australia has a long-standing relationship with Papua New Guinea and New Zealand is influential in several of the Polynesian islands. The fact that both are members of the South Pacific Forum and take its deliberations seriously has acted as a legitimating mechanism. So also is the belief that neither wish to assume a dominant role in regional affairs.

10.18 The small states in the Indian Ocean have been given security assistance by India and in the case of the Maldives in 1988 this proved crucial. France maintains an interest and involvement in the South West Indian Ocean. Its presence is not contested as it is in the South Pacific and so its influence is generally seen as benign. Security assistance has also been provided by Tanzania in the case of the Seychelles and now that South Africa has emerged from apartheid its role in Indian Ocean and Southern African security is likely to grow.

10.19 The continued military weakness of small states means that temporary assistance will almost certainly be needed to repel an invader (including any substantial mercenary action); to defeat secession (especially in outlying islands); and to quell or contain protracted urban riots, coup attempts, or any combination of disturbances, espe-cially if they are on any scale. In the absence of effective collective security through the UN or regional security mechanisms, small states will necessarily have to turn elsewhere for assistance, and even with regional involvement extra-regional help may be required. It will also be necessary on a more routine basis if effective intelligence networks are to be established and international crime combated and punished. The issue is therefore not so much the involvement of major and regional powers but the terms on which they do so and the extent to which they will remain committed to help them. In an age of competing resources small states will have to make every effort to encourage in such powers the development of a sense of voluntary responsibility for, and steward-ship of, regions in which they have had a beneficial presence.

Regional Security

10.20 In the *Vulnerability* report great stress was laid on the potential of regionalism for bolstering the operational capacity of small states and thus enhancing their security. This remains true, and it must be noted that over the last decade these states have made significant gains in this direction, in that regional networking and practical co-operation have been well developed at both the governmental and non-governmental levels. The governments are well aware of both the problems and the possibilities. Regionalism implies regional bureaucracy and services and the financing of these, especially where the agency is only made up of small states, has been a daunting problem for these states.

10.21 At the same time the current thrust in the Caribbean to develop an Association of Caribbean States, which will include all of the societies of the wider region, is an example of a renewed commitment to regionalism. Another is the Indian Ocean Rim Initiative which has attracted membership from 14 states and yet another the widening and deepening of the Southern African Development Community. While much of this has been impelled by globalisation there has also been a security component, either implied or prior to such developments and it is clear that regional programmes in security are likely to grow in number.

The Caribbean

10.22 In 1982 the Eastern Caribbean states, including Barbados, created, through a Memorandum of Understanding, a Regional Security System (RSS) involving a force constituted by mixing military, coastguard and police units. The RSS played a supporting role in the Grenada events of 1983, in Trinidad in 1990 and in Haiti in 1994. In 1996 the arrangement was upgraded into a treaty. The treaty specified that the RSS should have contingency plans for assisting member countries in national emergencies i.e. including drug interdiction, marine pollution, search and rescue operations and natural disasters. The emphasis on these activities is in accordance with a shifting perception of threat which in the early years was directed more at political instability and mercenary activity.

10.23 When it was first established the RSS attracted significant technical and material support from the United States, Canada and Britain, but this has declined significantly in the post-Cold War years. Since regional governments are also experiencing acute budgetary pressures the RSS is faced with major operational constraints. Nevertheless, RSS forces have been deployed annually since 1985 in military training

---

exercises and the number of regional and extra-regional countries involved have grown in recent years. There is clearly a need for such a security system and as an imaginative, low-cost example of self-help the RSS deserves sustained international support.

The South Pacific

10.24 In the South Pacific there has been a deepening of the regional security arrangements in a voluntary collective effort involving the two regional powers as well as the small states. Security arrangements depend very much on regional networking and co-operation and on ad hoc arrangements for peacekeeping forces.

10.25 In respect of illegal movement of arms and drugs, an awareness of increased permeability to criminal activities has led the SPF to take measures to deepen regional co-operation. Thus, in 1988, they established a Regional Security Committee which has, as one of its main responsibilities, the developing of a common approach to the control of weapons throughout the region. In 1995 the Forum also agreed on establishing 'Regional Support Arrangements' and ordered the development of appropriate mechanisms. The Honiara Declaration of Law Enforcement Co-operation (1992) is another example of increasing regional co-operation and has focused on legislative drafting assistance, improvements to the drug enforcement capabilities of regional police and customs agencies, and assistance to regional prisons and immigration to establish specialist regional fora.

The Indian Ocean

10.26 As noted earlier, regional organisation among small states in the Indian Ocean is weak. There are numerous regional organisations on the littoral involving Africa, the Middle East, South and South-East Asia, most of which were either products of the Cold War or political and economic co-operation following decolonisation. The new post-Cold War security landscape and new global economic agendas, however, are providing opportunities for developing new regional associations which may directly or indirectly enhance the security of the small Indian Ocean states.

South Africa

10.27 The SADC has recently taken a decision to transform the Frontline Group of States into an Association of Southern African States with specific security responsibilities. The intention is to proceed slowly and the most likely areas for regional security co-operation are diplomatic co-ordination, joint mechanisms for preventing and combating crime, exchanges of intelligence, and measures to curb drug trafficking and illegal immigration.

10.28 In 1993 the Organisation of African Unity (OAU) created a 'Mechanism for Conflict Resolution, Management and Prevention' (CRM) to deal with the growing problem of conflict in Africa, both internal and external. The CRM is guided by the principles of sovereignty and non-interference and functions on the basis of the consent and co-operation of the parties to a conflict. The primary emphasis is on anticipating and taking action to prevent the outbreak or escalation of a conflict and hence avoid the need to resort to complex and expensive peacekeeping operations which African states would find difficult to finance. The creation of the CRM has been welcomed by the international community as a whole.

Nuclear weapon free zones

10.29 Many small states have been active in opposing nuclear weapons. One measure they have taken in their region is to promote zones of peace or nuclear weapon free zones. The first moves in this direction were taken in Latin America with the conclusion of the Treaty of Tlatelolco in 1967 which established a nuclear-free zone. The idea of a 'zone of peace' was then promoted by some states in the Indian Ocean where it was directed at constraining and removing superpower competition. It has failed to make much headway. More successful has been the conclusion of the Treaty of Rarotonga in 1985 establishing a nuclear-free zone in the South Pacific and the signing of the Treaty of Bangkok in 1995 and the Pelindaba Treaty in 1996 which, respectively, have established nuclear weapons free zones in South-East Asia and Africa. A number of Commonwealth small states have already signed the Comprehensive Test Ban Treaty. Commonwealth Heads of Government have expressed their support for the establishment of nuclear-free zones based upon arrangements freely arrived at by all states in the regions concerned. They have also expressed support at Auckland for the Comprehensive Test Ban Treaty as a major step toward strengthening the nuclear non-proliferation regime and efforts for global nuclear disarmament, with its ultimate goal of the elimination of nuclear weapons.

Recommendations

10.30 In line with recommendations advanced in the *Vulnerability* report (see Annex), we reiterate the proposition that small states will need to address military and political security at several levels. We also acknowledge that small states will need to develop flexible multi-purpose programmes that promote internal cohesion as well as meet external threats. Finally, we underline the importance of developing effective intelligence and law enforcement capabilities to combat and punish international crime.

10.31 Small states which maintain a defence establishment are best served when that establishment is configured to carry out a diversity of functions including development projects and disaster relief. **Small state defence forces need to liaise closely with other government agencies and to acquire a range of paramilitary skills.** They can also gain from being part of a regional security programme when that programme relates primarily to the needs and concerns of small states within a distinctive regional setting. This is an important qualification as regional security has assumed greater prominence with the end of the Cold War and regional powers may have an agenda distinctly different from that of smaller states.

10.32 **Small states need to be mindful of the position of global powers.** The *Vulnerability* report cautioned against bilateral defence arrangements with a foreign power, seeing it as an option only in the last resort and only if a small state is under a real military threat from an identifiable enemy. This continues to be sound advice and is particularly pertinent to the present when the future shape of the international system is so unclear. At the same time there are many areas of overlapping interest between small and global powers, particularly in detecting and combating global crime. In such instances there is a case for **small states to actively seek the support of global powers to provide appropriate security assistance, subject to safeguards concerning national sovereignty.**

10.33 As already noted, small states tend to be more democratic than larger states and to have a good record on human rights. But as can also be shown small states can be at risk from personalist ambition and petty tyranny which is difficult to counter or redress given the pervasiveness of politics in small states and the relatively larger role of government in social and political affairs. **Small states must ensure that mechanisms are in place to limit would-be dictators and to support democratic processes.** A number of these were recommended in the *Vulnerability* report and we endorse them as practical measures which will promote internal cohesion (see Annex).

10.34 We also note that issues of human rights and good governance are now part of the international development agenda. **Small states have a vested interest in ensuring their domestic regimes are politically acceptable apart from the intrinsic value of maintaining democratic and accountable government in accordance with the principles set out in the Harare declaration.** At the same time the conditionalities imposed by international agencies or donor countries through structural adjustment programmes or debt management can have deleterious consequences for social cohesion by widening the gap between rich and poor and limiting the range of free or subsidised services which are targeted at and of particular benefit to the disadvantaged. In the design and implementation of such programmes the particular place of government in small states needs to be recognised and particular care taken over the implementation of policies such as privatisation and public sector reform.

10.35 The phenomenal growth of international crime has impacted on all states but small states are especially vulnerable because of their geographical location and characteristics and because they have only limited interdiction capabilities. This particularly applies to the twin threats of drug trafficking and money laundering although other criminal activities such as smuggling, illegal migration and unlicenced use of exclusive economic zones remain as matters of concern. To combat such threats effectively small states necessarily rely on others, particularly in respect of intelligence, detection and prosecution. **Efforts to develop information networks and securing external assistance and training to enhance their self-reliant defence efforts should remain a priority of small states.**

10.36 The *Vulnerability* report drew attention to the efficacy of regional intelligence networks in providing a routine flow of information and intelligence. There have been developments in this area but experience has also pointed to limitations and in **respect of international criminal activity a wider strategy is required.** Small states have begun to address these matters through adherence to relevant international conventions such as the UN Convention against Illicit Traffic in Narcotic Drugs and Psychotropic Substances and the adoption into commercial practice and national law of recommendations made by the Financial Action Task Force on money laundering. Much, however, remains to be done.

10.37 There is a **special role for the Commonwealth** in this area. Recent meetings of Finance Ministers and law enforcement officers from Commonwealth countries have addressed these issues and the Commonwealth Secretariat has an active programme of technical support. Small states are especially reliant on such fora to inform themselves of the issues and to put their views across as there is a danger that their legitimate interests in establishing offshore financial sectors could be ignored by larger states seeking tighter international regulation. At the same time small states have a duty to themselves and others to ensure that compliance is effective. In most cases this will require considerable technical assistance which the Secretariat is well placed to provide given the resources to do so. We recommend that **priority be given by the Commonwealth Secretariat to practical measures to help small states combat drug trafficking and money laundering at national, regional and international levels.**

11

National Measures to Enhance Security Through Capacity-Building

11.1 The most important resource in a small state is its people. Security and development in a small state will not be possible unless particular attention is paid to human development. In the words of a recent Commonwealth Secretariat report: 'The experience of countries with limited land and natural resources, like Japan, Hong Kong, the Netherlands or Singapore, bears ample testimony to the fact that the real prerequisite for a country's economic growth and development lies in the skills, enterprise and industriousness of its population. Human resource development does not conflict with the pursuit of economic development: rather it is the key. It provides a sound foundation for an uncertain future' (*Foundation for the Future* (1993) paragraph 12).

11.2 In the context of small states, this means attention to two vital components of capital: human capital and social capital. The importance of these two forms of capital for sustainable development were touched on in Chapter 7. They are discussed here in greater detail with a focus on how they can improve the capacity of small states. Capacity-building is an essential element in all small states. Our definition of security explicitly refers to it in the context of governing, protecting, preserving and advancing the state and its people. It is therefore about good governance as set out in the Harare Declaration as well as economic and social development. In all three, most Commonwealth states have a good and improving record which is to be welcomed as a positive contribution to human security and sustainable development. At the same time, small states, almost by definition, lack 'critical mass' in many areas. This particularly applies to acquiring and developing technology suited to their needs, which is of vital importance to small states in offsetting vulnerability and exploiting economic opportunity. To do this they will need help. International support is essential to provide small states with the skills they need to survive in the modern competitive world.

Human Capital

11.3 There is widespread agreement that 'human capital' is a critical element in the economic and social development of all societies. In essence, it refers to the 'quality' of human beings: an educated person is likely to yield social returns higher than a less educated person.

Someone who is in good health will similarly yield more than someone in poor health. Education and training are therefore the ingredients of human capital formation. Nutrition, primary healthcare, preventive medicine, clean water and adequate shelter and energy become the means of at least maintaining human capital and, ideally, of improving it. Nutritional improvement, for example, appears to be closely linked to increased life expectancy. In the same way, education, especially primary education for girls, is associated with reductions in infant mortality.

11.4 A general indicator of several basic elements of 'human capital' is given by the Physical Quality of Life Index (PQLI). This is calculated for each country, based on an average of life expectancy at age one, infant mortality and literacy rates, with 100 as the maximum possible score. Table 11.1 reports the PQLI for nearly all small developing states. It shows that most do well: 12 states have scores over 90, with the Caribbean as a region particularly well represented. Only four small states have scores below 50, all in Africa.

Education

11.5 One way of measuring the gains from human capital formation is to measure the social rate of return to education, and this can be done by measuring the difference between before-tax earnings of educated people and less educated people, and expressing this as a return to the costs of education in terms of the costs of providing educational services and the forgone income from being in education. Estimates suggest that such rates of return are extremely high in developing countries, especially in primary education where they exceed rates of return to other forms of capital investments.

11.6 Table 11.2 shows how small states compare to larger states in improving their indicators of education. It clearly indicates that small states have fared less well than large ones in expanding the proportions of the relevant populations in education or literacy programmes. Human capital, however, cannot be said to have declined since expansion is positive in all cases except small state primary school enrolment. And here the figures can, in part, be explained by sustained high rates of enrolment over the years. In 1993 these were at or above 100% for 18 Commonwealth small states.

11.7 While primary and secondary schooling are important, tertiary education and training are needed to provide the capacity for analysis, problem solving, and management at both general and specific levels. They also generate the cadres of technicians and other para-professionals who perform important tasks in project implementation, production and maintenance. Facilities for tertiary education are rudimentary

Table 11.1 The Physical Quality of Life Index for Small States (1993)*

	PQLI
Caribbean	
Antigua and Barbuda	93.3
The Bahamas	93.5
Barbados	97.0
Belize	90.5
Dominica	93.5
Grenada	90.2
Guyana	84.0
Jamaica	95.2
St Kitts and Nevis	86.6
St Lucia	90.8
St Vincent	88.0
Suriname	89.9
Trinidad and Tobago	92.9
South Pacific	
Fiji	88.4
Kiribati	76.4
Nauru	88.1
Papua New Guinea	61.5
Samoa	79.8
Solomon Islands	89.5
Tonga	82.6
Tuvalu	87.1
Vanuatu	76.2
Africa	
Botswana	77.7
Cape Verde	74.0
Djibouti	38.2
Equatorial Guinea	47.7
Gabon	58.6
The Gambia	35.7
Guinea-Bissau	36.7
Lesotho	68.9
Namibia	60.4
Sao Tome e Principe	79.7
Indian Ocean	
Comoros	59.4
Maldives	80.6
Mauritius	88.3
Seychelles	90.5
Mediterranean	
Cyprus	86.2
Malta	92.4
Asia	
Brunei Darussalam	92.8

*Commonwealth countries are shown in **bold**.

Source: Commonwealth Secretariat, *Small States: Economic Review and Basic Statistics* (1996)

in some small states and in the smallest among them there is a marked dependence on foreign technical assistance to fill the higher-level positions in the public service. There is clearly a need for small states to seek ways to improve levels of enrolment in tertiary education, which exceed 10% of the relevant age group in only a handful of countries. There is also a need to make training and education relevant. The orientation to 'practical' subjects varies considerably. In the Caribbean there is increasing emphasis on applied sciences including management; but in the South Pacific, because of a lack of resources to make the necessary curriculum changes, there is still a focus on humanities. **Widening the curriculum, supporting technical training and, where possible, promoting institutions to foster R&D, should be an urgent priority for small states.**

Table 11.2 Improvements in Human Capital 1980-1992
(Change in % of relevant population)

	Primary School	Secondary School	Adult Literacy
Small states	+0.00 [36]	+0.24 [31]	+0.26 [40]
Large states	+0.10 [30]	+0.92 [29]	+0.43 [?6]

Note: bracketed numbers refer to size of sample.

Source: calculations based on data in Commonwealth Secretariat,
Small States: Economic Review and Basic Statistics (1996).

11.8 Information technology can play a major role in improving quality and expanding the range of vocational and tertiary education and training. Such technology can be of particular importance in archipelagic countries where it is not cost-effective to set up higher institutes of education in each island. Distance learning is an approach which should be encouraged and supported, where necessary, with funds and expertise from other Commonwealth states.

Women and development

11.9 There are many reasons for focusing on the role that women play in sustainable development. Those that tend to be discussed in the literature on gender and development emphasise the vulnerability of women, their role as decision-maker within the household, their role as head of household in those societies where males migrate to urban areas to expand employment opportunities, their role as household manager, cook, child-rearer and labourer. All of these are wholly legitimate reasons for the focus on gender. While emphasis on gender issues may be justified as a correction of the unfairness of the roles that many women play, there is an efficiency argument that emphasises the special role that women play as a means of securing sustainable development. Put simply, ignoring women, or treating them as simply one more member of the household, risks unsustainable development. For women have special stores of knowledge and special skills without which many interventions in the economic system will fail. Some important features of this gender dimension of human capital are as follows. First, women tend to be closer to many natural resources than men. They are, for example, often responsible for the collection of water and biomass energy. This closeness generates a comparative advantage in understanding how water and biomass is best sustained as a natural resource. The same closeness argument applies to food security. Second, some economies are composed of small scale units: mountain ecosystems for example. Smallness tends to result in women-led management of the unit, and the resulting specialised knowledge of the workings of those ecosystems is a resource in itself. Third, in some ecosystems, women possess different knowledge to men, yet their inferior status tends to prevent them from having these skills recognised at the professional level. There are few women foresters, for example, yet women's knowledge of forestry is different in kind to that of men. Fourth, the migration of men to cities and as nomads means that many women are the effective managers of the land.

11.10 Gender-focused sustainable development policies will tend to emphasise the definition and enforcement of female rights to the land and to resources; better access to credit; better access to extension and professional training; participation in the design of projects and policies, and in the selection of technology; and careful assessment of the effects on women of any macropolicies. **In society as a whole, affirmative action should be taken to enable women and girls to access education, markets, credit, jobs, health care, legal services, decision-making fora, shelter, good sanitation and other resources.**

11.11 It is difficult to generalise about the position of women in small states. Where figures are available, there are large variations, within as well as between regions, in a number of important indicators: total fertility rate, as measured by number of children who would be born per female; literacy rate; and participation of females in the labour force. These are reported in Table 11.3. While they demonstrate that women are disadvantaged in a general sense, and that there are some common features to regions in respect of a more advantageous position for women in the Caribbean (indicated by lower fertility rates, higher literacy and greater participation in the work force) than in Africa, these appear not to relate specifically to size but reflect the general conditions of development obtaining in the region. In this sense, a specific programme addressing the particular position of women in small states is best carried through as part of a wider programme advancing the position of women generally.

Table 11.3 Women in Small States: Selected Social Indicators

	Total Fertility Rate	Literacy Rate %	Females in Labour Force %
Caribbean			
Highest	4.1 (Belize)	98 (The Bahamas)	49 (Grenada)
Lowest	1.7 (Antigua)	87 (Jamaica)	25 (Guyana)
Pacific			
Highest	5.0 (PNG)	88 (Fiji)	54 (Kiribati)
Lowest	2.1 (Nauru)	59 (PNG)	19 (Tonga)
Africa			
Highest	5.8 (Djibouti)	58 (Cape Verde)	42 (Lesotho)
Lowest	4.2 (Cape Verde)	20 (The Gambia)	24 (Namibia)
Indian Ocean			
Highest	6.7 (Maldives)	92 (Maldives)	42 (Seychelles)
Lowest	2.3 (Mauritius)	48 (Comoros)	22 (Maldives)

Source: Commonwealth Secretariat: *Small States: Economic Review and Basic Statistics* (1996)

Social Capital

11.12 Social capital refers to the stock of norms and values that bind a society together rather than dividing it to cause crime, family break up, civil strife and even war. Failure to understand individuals as social beings is therefore likely to threaten sustainable development as much as failing to 'get prices right' or pursuing poor structural adjustment policies. Sustainable policies must therefore involve an assessment of who the various actors are; what their stake is in one form of development rather than another; what the relationships are between these various stakeholders; what systems of resource rights (customary, communal, legal) exist; and what mechanisms exist for the voicing of concerns and views about development.

11.13 A parallel concern is expressed within the concept of human security. The idea was explored in the UN *Human Development Report* (1994) which identifies it as an all-encompassing concept including economic security, food security, health security, environmental security, personal security, community security and political security. The last two components are particularly important for small states, given that dispute and discord can quickly spread throughout society and become magnified into major challenges to social and political order.

11.14 Exclusion from the market, society and polity breeds insecurity and conflict. **Human security requires policies of participation, empowerment and integration.**

Employment

11.15 For the majority of people, the best form of market participation is through productive and remunerative work through self-employment or wage employment. This provides them with purchasing power for goods and services, a generally valued social role, and the opportunity to seek to influence decision-making in the workplace and beyond. The corollary is that unemployment contributes to poverty, social exclusion and political marginalisation.

11.16 The growth of unemployment in the developing world is therefore a worrying trend. It is particularly significant in a number of small states where employment opportunities are limited. In several of the Caribbean states, unemployment levels in excess of 20% to 30% of the work force have been common. Female unemployment rates are even higher, sometimes double the male rates. Youth unemployment has long been a factor stimulating emigration. Poverty has been on the rise in the region over the last two decades, despite the considerable economic growth witnessed nearly everywhere in the Caribbean in the1980s, and now affects some 38% of the population. The informal sector has absorbed workers who have lost jobs in the public and private sectors, but it is characterised by low productivity, limited access to credit, low income, poor working conditions and very few benefits.

11.17 There is an **urgent need for governments to create sufficient opportunities for productive employment.** Since most opportunities are likely to be generated by the private sector, the major thrust of policy must be to create an environment in which there are incentives for private enterprise. This includes support for small-scale enterprise through fiscal incentives and reform of the credit system as well as fair and stable macroeconomic policies. Other supportive measures are encouragement of service-based employment through investment in new skills and worker retraining. Where private enterprise fails to produce sufficient jobs, it may be necessary for the state to target interventions in favour of vulnerable groups and/or provide employment through public works programmes.

Empowerment

11.18 Empowerment of people is at the heart of human development. It involves fostering the enlargement of human capacities through promoting good health and educational opportunity; ensuring that people are able to develop and apply their knowledge and skills, and enhance their capabilities, through exercise of these attributes in work, leisure and civic settings; and creating institutional mechanisms which encourage active citizenship.

11.19 On the whole, small states provide a supportive social and institutional setting for the development of such capabilities. Small size, however, can create problems: connection rather than merit may govern recruitment to positions of authority and leadership; deference to hierarchy can discourage criticism and stifle initiative; excessive centralisation acts against devolution of authority and responsibility; and the small scale of organisations, public and private, limits career development. These constraints are recognised and inform much of the literature on public administration in small states. But there is always room for improvement, especially as government plays a large part in the delivery of services in small states. Programmes which sensitise small state administrators to issues of efficiency and accountability; and public service reforms which redress weaknesses in management arising from them, are to be encouraged. Training for administration must be provided nationally, although at a more senior level there is clearly a place for regional and international programmes.

11.20 Small states, in most part, also have a good record in providing access to the processes of government and the law; guarantees to freedom of belief, association and expression; and maintaining an open society in which rights as a citizen and employee can be asserted and defended against arbitrary practice. At the same time, small size can limit participation to the purely formal, e.g. participation in elections as a voter, but not as a politically active person outside election periods; or to excessive and multiple office holding by a few in government, civic associations and interest groups, thereby concentrating power in a small elite. Empowerment requires an active commitment by citizens to participate in government and the organisations of civil society. It mandates processes of consultation between government, community organisations, the private sector and individuals. These can help reconcile divergent interests and lend legitimacy to decisions reached, contributing to political stability and social cohesion. In all states, but especially small states, there is an **onus on government to provide the appropriate environment for active citizenship and to ensure that all groups are drawn into the conduct of public affairs.**

Social integration

11.21 Although small states are likely to be more socially cohesive than larger ones, governments need to ensure that no group is excluded from participation in the economic and political life of the country. One of the best ways to encourage social integration is to ensure all sections of society have access to basic educational opportunities that respect diverse cultures and traditions. Other measures include protection of minority rights through law, affirmative action in favour of the most disadvantaged and marginalised, and good governance.

11.22 Social spending can add to social integration. The proportion of national income devoted to education, health and social security and welfare in several small states is relatively high. In Barbados, Malta and Mauritius it exceeds 40% of government expenditure. The fact that all three have in the past achieved strong economic growth suggests that social spending underpins economic performance. It is therefore disturbing to note that in several small states the proportion of social spending has declined in recent years.

11.23 Good governance is an essential element of successful development. As noted earlier, the record in most small states is good. However, the growth of social inequality within many countries, including small states, puts stress on the social fabric and can lead to political challenges which threaten democratic political practices. Fortunately, such incidences have been few. But there is merit in recognising the value of anticipatory or preventive action in such circumstances. There are usually early warnings of impending social deterioration, as measured in declines in the various components of human security, which could and should trigger remedial action. While this is a delicate matter, since it touches on state sovereignty, **the Commonwealth is well placed to provide practical support and advice** in such circumstances, not as a substitute for national action to prevent crisis but as a complement to it.

Investing in Technology

11.24 Technology provides one of the means whereby the 'constant capital' rule for sustainable development could be relaxed. Improvements in technology mean that a given capital stock becomes more productive and hence capable of 'supporting' a larger level of human well-being. Technology can be used to meet various social goals: it might enable a larger population to be supported at the prevailing standard of living; it might enable a given population to enjoy a higher standard of living; or it might offset any declining productivity of extra capital stocks as capital is accumulated. One thing seems certain: without technological change, the chances of higher standards of living, whatever the population, are reduced.

11.25 The problem for small states is where does this technology come from? If small states have reasonably high incomes, it could be supposed that they should develop their own research and development programmes. But the economies of scale argument weighs against small states in this respect, as does the ease with which highly skilled individuals can migrate to those countries where financial rewards in research and development are highest. The issue of migration is especially important for small states. Migration results in increased overseas remittances, but the resulting income to the small state tends to be used for consumption goods, resulting in higher imports. The resulting increase in the small state standard of living may not therefore equal what could have been obtained had there not been out-migration, and the human resource base is depleted into the bargain. Migration also causes acute shortages in technological skills needed for development, making the country less competitive internationally; and can, when sustained over a long period in the smaller states, threaten the viability of the entire community, as the population fails to reproduce itself.

11.26 These considerations suggest that an appropriate technology policy is vital. Among its elements should be:

- associations of small states, where appropriate and geographically feasible, to overcome the economies of scale problem;

- areas for investment in new technology, targeted by diverting a proportion of government investment funds to develop that technology;

- incentives for private investment in the targeted technologies;

- an explicit policy of raising wages and salaries in the chosen sectors;

- technology trusts, using national and if possible concessional finance;

- a small states association to gather information on available technologies which will enhance the competitiveness of small states and contribute to sustainable development through biodiversity conservation and renewable energy.

11.27 Such a programme has clear 'chicken and egg' problems – some of the activities are designed to generate other parts of the package, but some small states have taken a clear lead in other areas of modern technology, e.g. in financial services. There is no persuasive reason why this example cannot be repeated for small states, other than those that are truly isolated.

Capacity-Building in Small States: The Commonwealth Experience

11.28 Many small states need support to undertake activities necessary to build up human and social capital for sustainable development. The Commonwealth Secretariat has an extensive programme of support to enhance human development and capacity-building in small states. While it is only one of a number of international organisations that can provide assistance, its focus on small states has given it a particular expertise which illuminates the type of measures small states need to take and the sort of help they can expect.

11.29 Expertise and training for public servants in small states has been provided in areas such as economic research techniques, property taxation, debt management, financial management, environmental impact assessment, tourism and the sustainable development of marine resources. Workshops have been convened to assist in maritime boundary delimitation and to build the capacity of small states to implement legislation to give effect to the various environmental agreements to which they are now party. Other areas where short-term training programmes have been designed to address skill shortages include economic and financial management, human resource development, privatisation, entrepreneurship development and general management programmes, as well as long-term postgraduate training in business administration and education planning.

11.30 In its provision of expertise to implement human resource development programmes, the Secretariat's aim has been to ensure that on-the-job training of counterparts is carried out to raise local capacities and ultimately reduce the requirement for technical assistance. In education it has helped to develop resource materials on the decentralisation of education systems; published or sponsored studies on the provision, management and distinctive nature of education in small states; enhanced, through training, the capacity of education ministries to deal with the financing of education; organised a workshop on examination systems in small states; supported the professional development (through distance learning) of teachers from small remote islands; and the University of Malta's six-month diploma in Educational Planning and Management for Small States. With the close collaboration of the Commonwealth of Learning, it is providing assistance with the development of distance education in the Caribbean and the South Pacific.

11.31 Commonwealth networks to exchange information and experiences on best practices in Civil Service reform have proved to be highly effective and have involved senior officials from a spread of small states. This complements a focus on developing capacity whenever possible at regional level. The Secretariat has signed Memoranda of

Understanding with CARICOM and the South Pacific Forum and collaborative links have been established or strengthened with a variety of regional or sub-regional agencies to enhance capacity in fields such as public sector management, information technology, tourism and insurance.

11.32 Women and youth have benefited in a variety of ways. The Secretariat has assisted small states with the development of policies on women, the strengthening of national women's machineries, and the training of senior policy-makers in the integration of gender concerns in national policies and programmes. Several small states benefit from the wide range of activities of the Commonwealth Youth Programme and its Regional Centres. Assistance has been given in developing youth policies, training youth leaders and providing seed funding for small enterprises created by young people.

11.33 While these programmes and projects improve the capacity of small states to manage their own affairs, it is unlikely that individually any of them will ever have a sufficient critical mass of skills to provide the comprehensive range of services obtainable in large developed states. The need for regional and international support to provide additional resources remains essential.

12

Enhancing the Role of Small States in the International System

The Position of Small States in the Global Context

12.1 When the framers of the Charter shaped the UN, it is clear that there was no expectation that the organisation would have, as it ultimately did, so many small states as full and equal members, and so there were no special provisions in the Charter to accommodate these states in one way or another. Indeed a striking difference between the UN and the League of Nations is that this earlier organisation featured a particular concern about the status and security of the small states of the day – those of Europe – and made specific provision to assist and protect them.

12.2 In the era of practically perpetual peace which was envisaged in 1945, it was not thought necessary to provide specially for the few small states then existing, since they were not seen to be at risk. It must be noted that even after the Cold War had started this perspective remained the same and that this continued to be the outlook when, through the decolonisation process, large numbers of small states joined the international community. These states were admitted as equal members of that community but their inability to provide for their own security was shown in time to be a fundamental weakness which called in question their status as sovereign states. But the assumptions of the Charter, which explained in part the emergence of these states, were that there would be a secure international community and effective provisions for collective security and mutual welfare. When in their early years, in a few cases, security challenges did occur they were manageable and there was no conception of a generic problem for small states in general.

12.3 This has meant that small states themselves have had to work hard to bring their problems to the attention of the international community. They have shown some diplomatic skill in doing so. In the first blush of independence these states were keen to play their part as members of the international community and many established sizeable foreign ministries. Most of these services have since either been cut back or, at best, not grown. There also has been a reduction in the size and style of the diplomatic accommodation abroad. The cutbacks have not been because of basic overstaffing but the result of financial constraints. This is regrettable as their need for adequate numbers of skilled representatives in the global marketplace to monitor developments and advocate their concerns is greater than ever given the large number of new state actors competing for resources in the international arena.

12.4 In international organisations small states have exhibited some skill and influence in conference diplomacy. Their numbers mean that their votes are often important in the work of these agencies, including those at the regional level. While the end of the Cold War has undoubtedly drastically reduced the negotiating space of many 'Third World' actors, the accumulated knowledge of these states can still stand them in good stead in international agencies which remain important arenas for these states to seek to secure security benefits and to further international harmony.

12.5 Through developing their expertise small states have already made signal contributions to world order, as in the pivotal role of Malta to the development of the new Law of the Sea, of Cyprus in advancing the adoption of the notion of peremptory norms of international law in the Law of Treaties, and of Trinidad and Tobago in the nascent International Criminal Court. These are areas where the newly created legal regimes can contribute to the welfare of small states, and thus are examples of an enlightened self-interest while serving the international community. Other issues on which small states have been very supportive of measures which build world community and improve welfare are the environment, disarmament, land mines, equality of gender and race, and human rights. By continuing and upgrading their contributions in such areas small states can make a vital contribution to building the sort of world in which their existence and status would not be questioned.

12.6 However, the ability of small states to maximise their roles in the international arena is severely hampered by their inability to participate fully at international meetings of importance to them, and by their limited capacity in accessing relevant information and data over a wide range of matters which impinge on their security. There is both a massive increase in available information and more decisions to be made in a busier world. There is also a need to make decisions in a faster time frame. Modern communications technology probably can help this problem significantly and it is an area worthy of some priority.

12.7 In general terms, Commonwealth small states will have to think very carefully about which aspects of international engagement are critical to them and which are not. The issue of ACP–EU consultation and negotiation regarding a successor agreement to the current Lomé Convention has been considered earlier. Experience in the last decade, and present and unfolding circumstances, suggest four other areas in which particular efforts should be made: the development of international law; the establishment of regimes within the WTO; reform and revitalisation of the UN; and support for the Commonwealth.

International Law

12.8 The definition of security advanced in this report highlights the need for small states to advance their interests within the framework of international law. In spite of spectacular infringements of international law, of which small states have been victim, international law has been growing in importance as an essential element in world order. The norm in the international community is one of compliance by states with rules which comprehend an ever growing variety of international transactions, which are themselves the inevitable product of the intensification of interdependence between nations.

12.9 Small states as weak powers stand to gain from an international system in which regimes and institutions are among the cornerstones of state interaction. An international regime is a set of rules, norms and procedures around which the expectations of actors (e.g. states or international organisations) converge in a certain issue area (e.g. trade, the environment or disarmament). The convergence of expectations mean that participants in the international system have similar ideas about what rules will govern their involvement and this in turn shapes their behaviour toward co-operative outcomes in which the benefits of mutual interest are paramount. When regimes are embedded in institutions like the IMF or the GATT international order is advanced.

12.10 One of the most important regimes for small states has been the adoption and entry into force of the UNCLOS. This has added considerably to the responsibilities of small states as at the same time it has increased their material interests. The territorial seas and archipelagic waters over which small states enjoy sovereignty now extend over thousands of kilometres, some of which were previously high seas, whilst the EEZs over which they may exercise sovereign rights are many times greater. The consequences of these changes, in the eyes of many, have been to transform some small island states from resource-poor to resource-rich nations. There is an element of truth in this, although the point may easily be exaggerated. The issue of resolving sovereign disputes regarding entitlements to the zones of maritime jurisdiction in accordance with the law acquires special significance. The rights to resources do not necessarily mean their effective exploitation. The high capital costs of deep water fishing, oil and gas exploration and sea-bed mining have held back their development and to date most returns to small states have come from licence fees paid by foreign fishing fleets. There is also the question of security. The size of EEZs are such that it is impossible for small states to police them effectively, even when given support by regional powers to do so. Small states have therefore had to rely on voluntary compliance by states as the only plausible means to reap benefits from the EEZs. In such a situation the obligation of compliance with international law by states is of considerable value.

12.11 Another area of international law of direct interest to many small states has been the activity of mercenaries. A Convention on the Elimination of Mercenaries in Africa was adopted by the OAU and a Regional Convention on the Suppression of Terrorism has been concluded by SAARC. The UN has adopted an International Convention Against the Recruitment, Use, Financing and Training of Mercenaries but ratification has been slow, particularly by some of the major powers whose support is vital if mercenary activity is to be outlawed.

12.12 There is also the question of neutrality. This has two meanings in international law: referring either to a specific situation in which a state adopts a status of neutrality with respect to a specific conflict, or a status which a state seeks to enter into permanently with the concurrence of other states. Small states have pursued neutrality in both senses. The outstanding example of the first is that many are members of the Non-aligned Movement (NAM). While there is a clear distinction between the legal status of neutrality and the political expression of non-alignment, the NAM has served the interests of several small states very well: specifically Belize, Cyprus and Guyana who have used the NAM to condemn aggression and gather diplomatic support in defence of their territorial integrity. An example of the second is Malta which has declared neutrality, written it into its Constitution and had it recognised by neighbouring and other states. Malta continues to attach great importance to its declared policy of neutrality and to advocate it as a policy suitable for small states. The status of neutrality would be enhanced by recognition by the UN Security Council. The *Vulnerability* report drew attention to this possibility, and despite the difficulties surrounding the adoption and recognition of neutrality for small states, felt it was an option worth exploring, a view shared by the authors of this report.

12.13 All states, but particularly small states, benefit from the general prohibition on both the actual use of force and the threat to use force in international relations as set out in Article 2(4) of the UN Charter. It outlaws not only recourse to war but any threat or use of force that is against the territorial integrity or political independence of another state or that is otherwise inconsistent with the purposes of the UN.

The principle contained in Article 2(4) has been cited by the Security Council, amplified in resolutions and declarations of the General Assembly, upheld by the International Court of Justice, and reaffirmed by the international community. They are, to this extent, widely held in the international system, providing an international legal basis for small states to seek prompt and effective action in the UN should they be subject to aggression.

12.14 The Commonwealth, as a principal legal system based on common law, could play a greater role in the international legal field to the benefit of its small state members.

The World Trade Organisation

12.15 The WTO provides a rules-based multilateral trading system. All members have rights and obligations. This is important for small countries since potentially they can defend their interests and influence the evolution of the organisation. It is an advance on a system of bilateral commercial relations based on economic and political power but only if small countries (and developing countries) can make their voices heard and participate fully in its operations. This will not be easy for two reasons.

12.16 Twenty-three Commonwealth small states have joined the WTO and applications from three others are currently pending. Few of these countries can afford to maintain a permanent office in Geneva and those that do accredit their representatives to the other major international organisations which are based there. Yet in the WTO alone the average number of meetings is now 46 a week. It is impossible for small states to cover them effectively unless they co-ordinate their efforts and work out a practical division of labour. Joint representation at the regional level offers an avenue to pursue this.

12.17 Second, the agenda of the WTO is substantial. To begin with there are numerous areas which have built in reviews and negotiations which will be important for small states. These include multilateral negotiations for liberalisation on trade in services under GATS; the continuation of the reform process under the agreement on agriculture; and review of the agreements on TRIMs and TRIPs, as well as recommendations in a number of areas including rules of origin. New issues have also been introduced including investment and competition policy. These will have to be covered alongside negotiations simultaneously being conducted with the EU in respect of Lomé, as well as with regional and sub-regional organisations.

12.18 In short, there are likely to be serious problems of human and technical capacity to cover these negotiations in sufficient depth, let alone achieve an effective policy synthesis across sectors and between various sets of negotiations. This problem has been recognised within the WTO and the UN Conference on Trade and Development (UNCTAD), but so far no proposals for assistance aimed specifically at small states, as distinct from developing states, have been advanced. Small states will therefore need to grasp the nettle themselves. In some respects this is already being done at a regional level, but it may be necessary to go beyond this to co-operate more closely in the WTO itself. The services of a trade policy expert based in Geneva have already been made available to small states under a Commonwealth programme. The possibilities of establishing a Joint Office along the lines of that at the UN in New York could be useful. Small states could also benefit from seeking closer integration of the WTO into the UN system where they would have the chance to influence policy in a broader context.

The United Nations

12.19 For small states, the best guarantee of their security is a universal collective security system prepared to resist aggression on their behalf. Therefore small states have always supported efforts to develop the United Nations into a truly effective world security agency. They have also placed the issue of small state security on the agenda of the General Assembly and the Security Council and have been active in promoting the work of the many agencies of the UN, particularly on the environment.

12.20 As noted earlier, the Maldives in 1989 piloted a resolution through the UN which was co-sponsored by 54 other states and adopted by consensus. The resolution entitled 'Protection and Security of Small States' called for international recognition of the vulnerability of small states and appealed to the international community to assist small states to strengthen their security. The resolution also called for the Secretary-General to play a wider role in accordance with Article 99 of the Charter which empowers the Secretary-General to bring matters which may be a threat to international peace and security to the attention of the Security Council. The Maldives followed this up with a Workshop on the Security of Small States in 1991 (attended by nine Commonwealth small states and several regional organisations) which recommended the establishment of a UN rapid response force to be under the direct control of the Secretary-General and which would be used to meet the security threats of small states at their request.

12.21 The report of the Secretary-General on the 'Protection and Security of Small States' was tabled in 1991. Twenty-two states submitted memoranda, eight of which were Commonwealth small states. The Security Council also discussed the issue. No common view emerged although it was recognised that because of their intrinsic characteristics, small states might need a special measure of support. This was reconfirmed in Resolution 46/43 of the General Assembly in 1991 which also stressed the importance of strengthening regional security arrangements. In 1994 the Secretary-General reported again on small state security. Memoranda were received from seven states, two of which were Commonwealth small states. Of note, is that in the discussions on the Security Council, the representatives of the European Community and the United States stressed that they would not agree to making any distinctions among states with regard to their security, maintaining this was unnecessary since the UN was based on the sovereign equality of states and provided for the security of all. The report therefore spoke in terms of establishing a general climate of support which would benefit small states, alongside developing particular security support in regional organisations. A further resolution (GARes 49/31) in favour of the protection and security of small states was passed in December 1994.

12.22 The Maldives initiative has been useful in clarifying positions but clearly limited in its outcome. Small states have therefore been more inclined, of late, to put their effort into reform of the UN. The proposal in 1992 by the then Secretary-General, Dr Boutros Boutros-Ghali in 'Agenda For Peace' on the need to establish a 'Conflict Early Warning System' in his office would certainly be welcomed by small states as important. At present the Secretariat offers advice and assistance on request and monitors on an ad hoc basis. Small states have also been concerned about any attempts to run the UN through a consortium of great powers and have therefore urged that UN reform should focus on more accountability and transparency. To date, for example, only five Commonwealth small states have served on the Security Council – Botswana, Jamaica, Malta, Mauritius and Trinidad and Tobago. It is the view of some small states that constitutional amendments to the Charter should consider the possibility of entrenching in the Security Council representation reflecting the large number of small member states. However, this has not been taken up by any of the proposals for reform which have attracted any significant measure of support.

12.23 The reform of other parts of the UN system to reflect the interests of small states is more likely to be successful. A model in this regard is the creation of AOSIS established at the end of the Second World Climate Conference in 1990 to raise awareness of the vulnerability of small island states to environmental threats. The membership of AOSIS includes all the Commonwealth SIDS. An early success was the identification of, and acceptance of, the need for a special programme for small island developing states which was set out in Agenda 21 and agreed at the UNCED in 1992. Subsequently the Global Conference on the Sustainable Development of Small Island Developing States was held in Barbados in 1994 which adopted a Programme of Action to be be co-ordinated by the UN. More recently, AOSIS has sought the adoption of a Protocol to the UN Framework Convention on Climate Change which proposes the adoption of a tougher regime cutting the emissions of greenhouse gases by developed countries by 20% by 2005, using 1990 as the baseline.

12.24 AOSIS points to the value of co-operation and co-ordination among small states wherever possible, and particularly in the UN system. The practice of regional representation within it gives small states the opportunity to raise their profile and exercise leadership on behalf of the region. The principle of rotation for selection to such positions allows small states to anticipate and prepare for office. It is to be commended and small states should seek its general acceptance within the UN system. They should also explore, more than they do at present, the adoption of common positions in UN agencies such as UNCTAD and the World Health Organisation, and the prosecution of common interests on major issues such as disarmament. The success of the South Pacific Forum in promoting the end of nuclear testing, and in another context of securing the reinscription of New Caledonia on the UN List of Non-Self-Governing Territories in the face of intense pressure by France, stands as an example of what small states can achieve collectively.

The Commonwealth

12.25 As the only major international agency where the majority of members are from small states, the Commonwealth has a unique role of advocacy in the global arena on behalf of those members. It also has a substantial technical programme in support of their development and a wide range of other activities of particular and of general interest to small states. The Commonwealth Secretariat has a comparative advantage in dealing with a wide range of small states' issues and is widely recognised by international and regional agencies for its expertise.

12.26 The Secretariat's assistance to small states is largely determined by mandates from governments and individual country requests. Hence the sectoral distribution of assistance reflects the priorities of small states themselves along with the ability of the Secretariat to respond to their needs. Five programmes have accounted for most spending: economic and social development, including sectoral policy assistance; human resource development; administrative and managerial reform; promotion of fundamental political values of the Commonwealth, including electoral assistance; and economic management, including economic policy advice. In the last few years total assistance has amounted to around two-thirds of the expenditure of the Commonwealth Fund for Technical Cooperation.

12.27 The establishment of the MGSS in 1993 has provided a forum for keeping a focus on small state concerns and the implementation of action plans. It is complemented by a Commonwealth Consultative Group on Small States (CGSS) composed of senior officials which was established in 1994 and supported by the Commonwealth Secretariat Task Force on Small States which was set up in 1995 to co-ordinate work within the Secretariat. The arrangements and programmes of work established by these groups was endorsed at the CHOGM in 1995.

12.28 Three areas of work have been identified by the MGSS and CGSS as being of particular importance. They are the sustainable development of small states, with a focus on environmental issues; small states and the international trading system, with an emphasis on economic questions; and the security of small states, which has addressed political and security issues broadly defined. The entire range of the Commonwealth Secretariat's work is comprehended by these programmes which address important issues such as capacity-building and human resource development within small states, as well as the provision of technical and policy advice through the preparation and dissemination of expert reports on areas of work identified as significant to them. Recent initiatives to develop closer relations with regional organisations through the conclusion of Memoranda of Understanding with the SPF and CARICOM have also added to the significance of the work of the Secretariat.

12.29 In addition, the Secretariat has been involved in the administration of the Joint Office for Commonwealth Permanent Missions to the UN (Joint Office) since it was established in 1983 with four members. Now nine Commonwealth small states use its facilities. In a review of the Joint Office undertaken in 1996 the users noted that it was critical to the conduct of their international relations at the UN. The review also concluded that the philosophy behind its creation remained valid and that it continued to fill a purpose.

12.30 A highlight of Commonwealth diplomacy and conflict resolution is the extensive 'good offices' work of successive Secretaries-General who have effectively exercised this capacity for quiet diplomacy in a number of political crises in small states. Recent instances have been in Lesotho and in Papua New Guinea. Allied to this is consensus building in its widest sense. The Commonwealth has observer status at the UN General Assembly and the Secretary-General has explored issues of international peace and security with the UN Secretary-General and supported him in his search for a settlement in Cyprus.

Recommendations

12.31 With the end of superpower conflict there is some hope that rules for a disciplined and universally acceptable international order are gradually being developed and that, within these, accommodation can be made for the particular concerns of small states. Whether or not such an order will evolve is a matter for the international community at large, but small states collectively and individually have a part to play. Their common interest is in creating an orderly world in which the asymmetries of power are tempered by international institutions. **Small states should use their number and in many cases their good example to strengthen multilateral co-operation as the basis for developing a more humane and equitable global order.**

12.32 To this end **small states should be proactive in promoting international law and the regimes which are being fashioned in a multitude of areas.** Regimes foster a co-operative international order and provide a web of legal and institutional support addressed to the multi-faceted problems relevant to small state security. While it would be ideal to establish a regime specific to small state security it would be unlikely to address the needs of all small states. A better route is to determine those which are of special relevance and promote their endorsement and ratification by the overwhelming majority of states in the international community. Accordingly, **we recommend that a study be undertaken to determine which regimes are of particular importance to small state security with a view to their early ratification.** The study should also determine areas in which future regimes could be promoted as of interest to small states with a view to examining the feasibility of small states taking a lead in their introduction.

12.33 **Small states must be supportive of reform of the UN and its emergence as the central institution for global governance.** In furthering this process small states need to be mindful of their strengths and their weaknesses as well as their particular interests. Small states have contributed peacekeeping forces to the UN but in reality their role is necessarily constrained by size. Likewise small states have been supportive of measures for disarmament and demili-tarisation but their voice is weak and often unheard. On security issues, traditionally conceived, small states are unlikely to make headway. Where they can make a difference is **on the growing economic, environmental and humanitarian agendas. Small states should ensure that they are at the centre of discussion and proposals for reform** in these areas. They should also seek to establish mechanisms within the UN system which ensure their representation on a regular and orderly basis. This approach obviously requires the maximum presence of small states at the UN. **We recommend that Commonwealth small states not permanently present at the UN examine the benefit of joining the Joint Office.**

12.34 We acknowledge the role the Commonwealth has played in supporting small states. It is not matched by any other international institution in advocacy, policy advice and practical assistance. We would wish to see this continue and if possible be enhanced. This means additional resources and extra burdens, particularly on the Commonwealth Secretariat. The mechanisms within it for monitoring and reviewing small state assistance appear to work well and we make no recommendation for change. Similarly, the process of identifying projects and programmes of interest to small states as being driven by small states takes account of their special needs. However, in view of the importance of policy co-ordination identified above we believe that there is a **need to strengthen present arrangements within the Secretariat to co-ordinate programmes of assistance to small states, including developing relations with NGOs.** The existing Secretariat Task Force could have a number of tasks but central among them would be ensuring the concerns of small states are actioned into the opening years of the twenty-first century.

References

Bartelmus, P, Lutz, E and Schweinfest, S (1993) 'Integrated Environmental and Economic Accounting: a Case Study of Papua New Guinea' in E. Lutz (ed.), *Toward Improved Accounting for the Environment* (World Bank: Washington DC).

Bijlsma, L (1996) 'Coastal Zones and Small Islands' in Intergovernmental Panel on Climate Change (IPCC) *Climate Change 1995: Impacts, Adaptations and Mitigation of Climate Change – Scientific-Technical Analysis* (Cambridge University Press: Cambridge).

Briguglio, L (1995) 'Small Island Developing States and their Economic Vulnerabilities' *World Development* Vol. 23, No. 9, 1615-32.

Commonwealth Secretariat (1985) *Vulnerability: Small States in the Global Society* (Report of a Commonwealth Consultative Group).

Commonwealth Secretariat (1993) *Foundation for the Future: Human Resource Development* (Report of the Commonwealth Working Group on Human Resource Development Strategies).

Commonwealth Secretariat (1995) *Small States: Economic Review and Basic Statistics.*

Commonwealth Secretariat (1996) *Small States: Economic Review and Basic Statistics.*

Commonwealth Secretariat (1997) *Small States: Economic Review and Basic Statistics.*

IPCC (Intergovernmental Panel on Climate Change) (1992) *Global Climate Change and the Rising Challenge of the Sea* (Report of the Coastal Zone Management Subgroup, IPCC).

IPCC (Intergovernmental Panel on Climate Change) (1996) *Climate Change 1995: IPCC Second Assessment Report* (Cambridge University Press, Cambridge).

Sutton, P and Payne A (1993) 'Lilliput under Threat: the Security Problems of Small Island and Enclave Developing States' *Political Studies* Vol. XLI, No. 4, 579-593.

Turner, R K, Subak S and Adger N (1996) 'Pressures, Trends and Impacts in Coastal Zones: Interactions Between Socioeconomic and Natural Systems' *Environmental Management* Vol. 20, No. 2, 159-173.

Ullman, H (1983) 'Redefining security' *International Security* Vol. 8. No. 1.

United Nations Commission on Sustainable Development (1997) *Implementation of the Program of Action for the Sustainable Development of Small Island Developing States: Report of the Secretary General* (Economic and Social Council: New York)

United Nations Development Programme (1994) *Human Development Report 1994* (Oxford University Press: Oxford).

United Nations Disaster Relief Organisation (1990) *Preliminary Study on the Identification of Disaster-prone Countries Based on Economic Impact* (UNDRO: Geneva).

World Bank (1996) *Global Economic Prospects* (World Bank: Washington DC.)

Annex

Recommendations of the 1985 Vulnerability Report

The various measures advocated in Part III of our Report are set out below as formal recommendations. They are arranged in terms of the three levels at which they would be implemented: national, regional and international. However, since this is a study requested by Commonwealth Heads of Government, the recommendations specifically for Commonwealth action are presented separately from the other international measures. For ease of reference the measures within each group have as far as possible been organised under headings that reflect the main subject areas covered in Part III (Chapters 5-9); and the numbers in square brackets indicate the paragraphs where the proposals are discussed. The recommendations are numbered in a straight sequence, starting from No. 1 under the section on National Policies and Measures and ending with No. 79 under the Commonwealth section.

1. National Policies and Measures

A. Strengthening National Defence Capability

1. Small states should aim at establishing multipurpose and flexibly structured security forces, able to carry out a diversity of functions including development projects and disaster relief. Primary emphasis should be given to paramilitary skills. Governments should recognise the need for appropriate equipment and a high level of motivation and morale [5.13-5.15].

2. Well trained citizen forces or voluntary reserves could serve as a useful back-up to the regular security forces and increase the capacity to deter external territorial threats [5.16-5.17].

3. Governments should recognise the necessity of training and using professional security advisers spanning the fields of foreign, defence, economic and general internal policies, and of developing efficient organisational structures to harness their services [5.38-5.39].

4. Small states contemplating bilateral security arrangements with a larger power should give due weight to their regional implications and possible adverse political impact before reaching a decision, particularly if the larger power seeks base facilities. In general, formal defence arrangements with a larger power should be seen as an option to be

exercised only where a small state is under a military threat from an identifiable enemy [5.23].

5. Where appropriate, small states could consider formally declaring a status of neutrality consistent with international law and seeking to have it officially recognised, at least by neighbouring countries and possibly also by the Security Council [5.28; and see also No. 45].

6. There is a considerable role for external assistance in enhancing the self-reliant defence efforts of small states. The major areas for such assistance are training, intelligence, costly equipment (particularly in maritime areas), logistics facilities and infrastructure. Although bilateral technical assistance poses less risk than bilateral defence arrangements, care should be taken to avoid arousing suspicion within the region, and over-militarisation [5.51].

7. Immediate steps should be taken by small states to improve their access to a wide variety of information on developments and views affecting national security interests and to introduce or upgrade regular systems for the procurement and analysis of information from abroad, particularly of a diplomatic and security nature [5.37].

8. Small states could make much greater use of information available at the United Nations and its agencies, as well as in the Commonwealth Secretariat. They should also endeavour to develop or upgrade information exchange relations with other Commonwealth member countries [5.36].

9. While improvement of intelligence data and analysis is essential, small states have, of necessity, to be very selective in using their own meagre intelligence resources; emphasis should therefore be placed on regional co-operation [5.40; and see also under Section II].

10. Small states also stand to benefit considerably from bilateral arrangements with regional partners or other friendly states for exchange of intelligence [5.41].

B. Underpinning Economic Growth

11. Economic diversification could greatly help to reduce economic weakness and insecurity, and should be an important objective of small states [6.5-6.6].

12. Difficulties of economic diversification should not be allowed to encourage over-concentration on 'softer' development options and deter efforts to secure more stable and sturdy economic development. The latter will require high standards of administration and management to make the best use of limited economic opportunities and to avoid the pitfalls of sanctions associated with foreign investment [6.6-6.7].

13. Transnational corporations could assist the economic development of small states which must, however, be helped to overcome their weakness in dealing with these corporations [6.9].

14. A vigorous indigenous private sector can, in appropriate cases, contribute directly and through joint ventures to self-reliant development and to reducing the dangers from transnational corporations [6.10].

15. A special effort is needed to develop indigenous technological capacity, not only to improve research and development but also to assess and adapt imported technologies [6.11].

16. Small states, even when densely populated, could increase food and other agricultural production through intensive cultivation assisted by land reform and technical support. Food production, tourism and other service industries and manufacturing could add to traditional exports and provide scope for diversified development [6.12].

17. Small states should be outward-looking in their development policies, even though this increases exposure to external influences. Rapid, stable and self-reliant development can only be achieved through skilful exploitation of internal and external economic opportunities [6.13].

18. In marine development, small states should give priority to: drafting of national legislation covering all uses of ocean space, including the declaration of their EEZs; integration of the marine sector into the general development strategy; establishment of an administrative structure for marine development [6.24].

C. Promoting Internal Cohesion

19. Small states should constantly pursue policies aimed at engendering confidence in public institutions and fostering active involvement in the democratic process. Specific measures should be taken, where necessary, to improve parliamentary procedures and to provide research and administrative assistance for Members of Parliament [7.5].

20. Measures in the human rights area could include: encouragement or development of non-governmental institutions [7.8]; fostering freedom of expression through the development of independent media [7.9]; and provision of constitutional safeguards for the protection of human rights and an independent judiciary [7.11].

21. Given their limited human resources, small states need to develop an administration staffed by personnel who are skilled in more than one task relating to development management [7.16].

22. While they must remain open to new influences and techniques and retain the capacity to innovate, small states should nevertheless continue to protect their national identity and core values [7.17].

D. Diplomacy and Foreign Policy Management

23. It is vital for a small state to formulate co-ordinated foreign policy objectives and strategies that take fully into account the implications of being a tiny entity in the international arena. They should develop positive techniques of diplomacy to compensate for their limitations, including occasional judicious use of bold initiatives [8.15; specific pointers for consideration are set out in 8.16-8.20].

24. Small states belonging to the same geopolitical group should appreciate that co-ordination of foreign policy can assist them to maximise modest national diplomatic resources and provide a useful source of political support. Where they share a common view on certain foreign policy issues, it could also be advantageous for them to have regular consultations, formally or informally, to consider the desirability of establishing a co-ordinated position [8.21-8.24].

25. Since small states can maintain overseas missions only in a handful of countries, careful judgement is required in deciding on which states to focus. Full advantage must also be taken of membership of inter-governmental bodies, both regional and transregional, which provide a valuable alternative means of fostering bilateral relationships. Location of suitably skilled diplomatic personnel in posts advantageous to gathering information relevant to the national interest is of considerable value [8.3-8.5].

26. Small states should consider the advantage of playing an active and constructive role within the United Nations [8.12-8.14]. States confronted by a specific security threat from another country should appreciate that immediate recourse to the Security Council can sometimes help in warding off aggression [8.11]. They can also seek, through a systematic use of Assembly procedures and its subsidiary bodies, to mobilise majority support from the United Nations membership, including some of the major powers [8.9].

27. Small states should plan their participation in international activities on a highly selective basis, focusing essentially on issues closely related to their national interests [8.19].

E. Training Needs

28. It is recommended that small states adopt a more systematic policy of seeking training assistance for national/Civil Service personnel in

the various areas of action identified in the Report as essential for reducing their vulnerability. These are:

- paramilitary skills, disaster and famine relief, operations to counter smuggling, drugs and arms trafficking, and the monitoring and surveillance of EEZs [5.55-5.56, 6.6-6.7, 9.48-9.49];

- information and intelligence gathering and analysis [5.41];

- public administration and management [7.30-7.31];

- the skills required to promote the smooth functioning of the parliamentary and legal system as well as the effective promotion of human rights [7.29];

- the development of the media, including news agencies [7.9, 7.29];

- the use of technology applicable in the relevant economic sectors, including industrial and agricultural development [6.10-6.11];

- ocean management [5.55];

- the techniques of diplomacy and negotiation, both bilateral and multilateral levels [8.25]; attention is drawn to the need for studies to provide guidelines in the conduct of diplomacy for small states [8.31];

- the skills for dealing with foreign commercial enterprises, as well as for negotiating contractual arrangements [6.7-6.9].

29. Greater use should be made, not only at the bilateral level but also at the regional and transregional levels, of the diversity of established sources within the Commonwealth for providing training and assistance in all these spheres.

II. Regional Initiatives

A. Strengthening National Defence Capability

30. Where small states form a distinctive geopolitical group it might be appropriate for them to consider establishing their own regional security arrangements. These could also provide an institutional structure for formalising requests for assistance, either from a larger power or from an international organisation, at moments of crisis [5.31-5.34; and see also No. 75].

31. To assist small states' access to vital information affecting their security interests and improve their capacity for information analysis, two initiatives are recommended:

- establishment of regional facilities – e.g. data banks, documentation centres, news agencies and other media outlets – for collecting and disseminating relevant publicly available information [5.36].

- establishment of regional intelligence networks to provide a routine flow of information on external developments with important regional implications, on significant intraregional developments, and on the internal problems of the constituent states which could affect at least some neighbouring small countries. In island states regions the network should also be envisaged as a source for intelligence on activities such as fishing, smuggling, illegal immigration and the commercial use of the sea-bed. While distribution of intelligence information could be carried out through a regional centre or agency, the means of analysing this material should remain in the hands of the individual governments [5.42-5.50].

B. Underpinning Economic Growth

32. Regional co-operation remains of special significance for small states' efforts to expand economic opportunities and reduce weakness in external economic relations [6.14].

33. Apart from expanding trade opportunities, regional co-operation could support national efforts to improve infrastructure and develop productive enterprises. Areas in which regional co-operation requires support from the Commonwealth and other external agencies include: surveillance and development of marine resources, disaster preparedness and relief, higher education, research and development, sharing scarce and expensive skills and expertise, transport and development banking [6.15].

34. In utilising and protecting the marine environment, developing marine science and facilitating the transfer of marine technology, small island states should seek assistance to establish regional centres to support these activities and also endeavour to relate them to the Regional Seas Programme contained in the 1982 Law of the Sea Convention [6.25-6.26].

35. Creation of regional fishing enterprises is recommended as a means of helping individual states to meet the challenge of the distant-water fishing fleets of the industrialised countries [6.26].

C. Promoting Internal Cohesion

36. Where practicable small states should seek to strengthen democratic and human rights practices through regional mechanisms such as

election commissions and service commissions for key judicial, administrative and security posts. They might also contemplate voluntary recourse to regional and/or Commonwealth observers at particular elections and encourage the activities of relevant regional and international NGOs [7.4].

37. If the constituent countries so desire, regional parliaments could be established as an instrument contributing to harmony and stability and giving impetus to general co-operation [7.28].

38. The establishment of regional human rights courts or commissions is recommended for consideration [7.6-7.7].

39. Small states should co-operate in schemes for the regional pooling of experts, e.g. auditors, legal draftsmen, specialist surgeons, etc. Freedom of regional movement and flexible conditions of work would facilitate such schemes [7.26].

D. Training Assistance Arrangements

40. Establishment of regional training centres in the various specialised skills, including management and developmental administration, required by the small states within a particular region is strongly recommended [7.29-7.31].

E. Regional Consultations on Security

41. Informal regional colloquia on national and international security questions, attended by governmental and non-governmental representatives and organised at, say, two-yearly intervals, could be extremely helpful. Procedures for these meetings could be drawn up in consultation with the Commonwealth Secretariat which could also assist with their organisation [7.21].

42. Regional consultations between officials should also be held on a regular basis to exchange information and views on developments affecting security in the area and on common problems. Some of these consultations might usefully include officials from non-Commonwealth neighbouring countries. The Commonwealth Secretariat could help in arranging them [9.55].

III. Action at the Global Level

A. Political Measures at the United Nations

43. Wherever possible small states should utilise the facilities of the United Nations and the International Court of Justice, as well as other appropriate international bodies in pursuit of their security needs.

However, governments need to give urgent consideration to how best to support proposals currently under discussion at the United Nations to strengthen its capacity to maintain peace and security [9.4-9.8].

44. Whatever the outcome of these discussions the Secretary-General should, in any event, play a more active role in the spirit of Article 99 of the United Nations Charter. In particular he should, in cases of incipient and low-level security threats, consider responding positively to a request from a state, feeling itself under military threat from another state, for a mission to its territory. When it is not politically feasible for him to despatch such missions, he could at least send a personal representative or an official of the United Nations Secretariat to obtain a firsthand assessment of the situation [9.9-9.13].

45. The Security Council should consider giving official recognition to formal declarations of neutrality status which any small state may individually seek to register with it [9.14, and No. 5 above].

46. As an initial step towards establishing a special unit within the Secretariat to assist small member states, an official should be appointed to monitor developments in the United Nations affecting their interests. The relevant departments within the Secretariat should also be instructed to consider developing special programmes for small states [9.15].

B. International Economic Policies

47. The international community has a special obligation to provide an external environment which could assist small states in promoting self-reliant and stable development and in strengthening their economic independence. That environment does not now exist and the situation is being made worse by the current difficulties experienced in multilateral co-operation. Renewed commitment and support for multilateral co-operation would greatly assist in the adoption of specific international measures. Areas of special importance to small states are: trade liberalisation; official flows from multilateral and bilateral sources, in particular concessional flows; technical co-operation; balance of payments support, including export earnings stabilisation; disaster preparedness and relief [9.21-9.27].

48. The provision of special support for small states should be approached pragmatically through securing better international recognition of their problems and needs and through categorisation of small states, formally or informally, in specific areas as the need arises [9.24-9.25].

49. ECOSOC should review as early as possible the criteria for inclusion of countries in the Least Developed category to take account of the

special structural and developmental problems of small states [9.28].

50. Bilateral aid agencies should continue to recognise the special needs of small states for concessional capital. Multilateral provision is of special importance and international financial institutions must pay greater attention to these needs [9.29-9.30].

51. The World Bank should adopt more flexible criteria for graduating small states from its lending, especially from IDA. No small states should be graduated from IDA unless there is assurance of adequate access to alternative sources of finance. Transitional arrangements might be required to prevent adverse effects from an abrupt end to IDA lending [9.33-9.35].

52. The IFC should significantly extend its support to smaller projects. It should also assist regional and national development banks to expand their operations in this area. The latter should do more to provide venture capital for small projects [9.36-9.37].

53. The IMF should review the functioning of its Compensatory Financing Facility to improve its effectiveness in stabilising foreign exchange earnings, giving special attention to the needs of small states [9.40-9.41].

54. The agreement to establish a Common Fund for commodity price stabilisation should be implemented as early as possible. Its modalities should reflect the special interest of small states [9.43].

55. Small states should be freed from all limitations that apply to their access under the Generalised System of Preferences, and exempted from all organised marketing arrangements and voluntary export restraints. Small states should be excluded from the export restriction adopted in any renewed MFA [9.44-9.45].

56. The Codes of Conduct on relations between transnational corporations and host countries, which are under negotiation, are of special interest to small states and should be established early [9.38].

57. Increased international assistance should be given to small states to improve their vetting procedures and negotiating capacity in dealing with foreign business ventures [9.39].

58. International arrangements on disaster preparedness and relief measures should be considerably improved. Greater international assistance should be provided to strengthen national efforts; regional efforts should be encouraged and supported [9.48-9.49].

59. International institutions should be more supportive of regional co-operation arrangements involving small states [6.15-6.17].

IV. The Commonwealth Contribution

Mindful of the fact that the Secretariat has already initiated an extensive programme of assistance to small states in many spheres, we are of the view that the Commonwealth is especially well placed to take practical measures to help small states in promoting their security interests as well. The programme already encompasses a wide spectrum of support in the political, economic and social fields, and an expansion of the Secretariat's activities in these areas would contribute significantly to reducing small states' vulnerability. Small states' security problems and objectives should, however, be kept constantly in mind when formulating new projects or considering how best to respond to requests for assistance from their governments. The present programme can be adapted by making a more focused use of the existing institutions and procedures. There is also a need for additional assistance at the bilateral level, but, again, in many instances this will be largely a matter of building on existing aid and co-operation arrangements.

A. Extending the use of Commonwealth structures

60. The Secretary-General has been in an excellent position personally to contribute to the general promotion of small states' security interests and we would urge that he continues this role through quiet diplomacy on an on-going basis [9.57].

61. He has also been able to contribute to the resolution of disputes involving member countries. In furtherance of this role, with regard to a security crisis arising for a small member state, the Secretary-General might consider it advisable to initiate immediate consultations with that state and with the other member states in the region in order to determine whether there is any wish for pan-Commonwealth action. In certain circumstances it might also be appropriate for him to despatch a team at the request of a small state feeling itself under an external threat to its security [9.58].

62. Special meetings of small states specifically on economic and financial matters should be arranged when the occasion warrants. They would be particularly helpful if organised in preparation for upcoming major international negotiating conferences, and would assist the Secretariat in trying to ensure that small states' interests are adequately represented at these fora [9.56].

63. The Commonwealth Fund for Technical Co-operation should be enabled to respond to requests from small states for training assistance and consultancy services for projects of practical relevance to their security problems. As the Fund's terms of reference preclude it from

financing projects directly concerned with national security, we recommend that these be revised with a view to removing the restriction entirely, or at least in the case of the smaller member countries [5.54; 9.52].

64. Additional resources should be provided to enable the Commercial Crime Unit of the Secretariat to meet the increasing demand for its services, mainly from small states [9.68].

65. Small states' general training needs are listed in No. 28. These should be noted by the Secretariat/CFTC with a view to augmenting the training programmes where appropriate.

66. Member countries could likewise review the list of training needs in order to determine the level and type of additional training assistance they feel they are in a position to offer, either by expanding existing programmes or by offering new ones as may be appropriate.

67. In the sphere specifically of military, paramilitary and police training, where a number of permanent arrangements have already been established, there is also room for both wider and more intensive bilateral co-operation [9.61].

68. Member countries should take initiatives to increase the flow of intelligence information to and between small states [5.41].

69. Existing intra-Commonwealth bilateral defence co-operation programmes, which include the supply of military hardware and joint service operations, have proved their utility and should constitute a basis for expanded co-operation [5.51].

70. There have been occasions when a Commonwealth country has provided direct military assistance to a small member state at its request at a moment of crisis; this practice is worth maintaining [9.59].

71. The follow-up work on the establishment of a Commonwealth Risk Capital Facility being carried out by the Secretariat should pay particular attention to small states' needs and be completed as early as possible [9.67].

72. The Secretariat's capital markets programme should give increased attention to assisting small states to tap capital markets [9.64-9.65].

73. If a new round of multilateral trade negotiations is held, the Secretariat should arrange a meeting of small member states to discuss issues of special interest to them and also ensure that their interests are adequately represented in the negotiations [9.71].

74. Despite current budget stringency, the significant levels of Commonwealth bilateral aid to small states should not only be maintained but improved over time [9.29].

B. Specific New Measures

75. In the event that a particular group of small states decides to set up its own regional security force, Commonwealth resources should, wherever possible, be made available on both a multilateral and bilateral basis [9.60].

76. Commonwealth governments should consider with sympathy requests for ad hoc forces to assist member states facing acute security problems [9.59].

77. All Commonwealth governments are urged to use their good offices to discourage insensitive and irresponsible reporting about small states, at least by the media in their own countries. This concern should also be brought to the attention of the Commonwealth Press Union [5.35].

78. The successful Australian funded scheme providing a joint New York office for the permanent United Nations missions for four of the Commonwealth's very small countries should now be accepted as a permanent measure and undertaken as a collective Commonwealth obligation, including a minimal contribution by the beneficiary countries. Resources should also be made available for similar facilities for other regional groups of small states that might seek such assistance [9.53-9.54].

79. We would strongly urge Commonwealth Heads of Government to consider ways in which the United Nations can be utilised to promote action for advancing the security interests of small states and, specifically, how the measures advocated in this Report could be brought to the attention of the international community [9.16].

Members of the Advisory Group

Commonwealth Advisory Group for Updating the 1985 Vulnerability Report

Dame Eugenia Charles, *Chairperson*
Former Prime Minister
The Commonwealth of Dominica

Mr Andreas Jacovides
Former Senior Diplomat
Cyprus

Mr Natarajan Krishnan*
Former Senior Diplomat
India

Hon Ms Fiamé Naomi Mata'afa
Minister of Education
Samoa

Dr Edgar Mizzi*
Former Attorney-General
Malta

Mr Ken Ross
Senior Analyst, Department of Prime Minister and Cabinet
New Zealand

H E Professor Havelock Ross-Brewster
Ambassador of Guyana to Belgium and the European Community
Brussels

Mr Tim Thahane
Deputy Governor
Reserve Bank of South Africa
South Africa

Mr Taniela Tufui*
Chief Secretary and Secretary to the Cabinet
Tonga

---

* A member of the Commonwealth Consultative Group which prepared the 1985 *Vulnerability* Report.

Commonwealth Secretariat

The Hon Sir Humphrey Maud, KCMG
Deputy Secretary-General, Economic and Social Affairs

Mr Rumman Faruqi
Director, Economic Affairs Division

Mr Jon P Sheppard
Director, Political Affairs Division

Mrs Judith Pestaina
Special Adviser, Political Affairs Division

Dr Chris Easter
Deputy Director, Economic Affairs Division

Dr Jackson Karunasekera
Chief Economics Officer
Economic Affairs Division

Consultants

Dr Paul Sutton
Director, Centre of Developing Area Studies
The University of Hull

Professor David Pearce
Director
Centre for Social and Economic Research on the Global
Environment
University College, London

Abbreviations

ACP	African/Caribbean/Pacific countries – Lomé Convention
ACS	Association of Caribbean States
AOSIS	Alliance of Small Island States
APEC	Asia Pacific Economic Co-operation forum
CARICOM	Caribbean Community
CBI	Caribbean Basin Initiative
CGSS	Consultative Group on Small States – Commonwealth
COMESA	Common Market for Eastern and Southern Africa
CRM	Mechanism for Conflict Resolution – Organisation of African Unity
CSD	Commission on Sustainable Development – United Nations
ECOWAS	Economic Community of West African States
EDF	European Development Fund
EEZ	Exclusive Economic Zone
EU	European Union
FDI	Foreign Direct Investment
FTAA	Free Trade Area of the Americas
GATS	General Agreement on Trade in Services
GATT	General Agreement on Tariffs and Trade
GEF	Global Environment Facility – United Nations
GSP	Generalised System of Preferences
IDA	International Development Association
IDB	Inter-American Development Bank
IFI	International Financial Institution
IMF	International Monetary Fund
IOC	Indian Ocean Commission
IORARC	Indian Ocean Rim Association for Regional Co-operation
IPCC	Intergovernmental Panel on Climate Change
MFA	Multi-Fibre Arrangement
MFN	Most Favoured Nation
MGSS	Ministerial Group on Small States – Commonwealth
NAFTA	North American Free Trade Agreement
NGO	Non-Governmental Organisation
NAM	Non-Aligned Movement
OAS	Organisation of American States

OAU	Organisation of African Unity
OECS	Organisation of Eastern Caribbean States
ODA	Official Development Assistance
PQLI	Physical Quality of Life Index
R&D	Research and Development
RSS	Regional Security System – Eastern Caribbean
SAARC	South Asian Association for Regional Co-operation
SADC	Southern African Development Community
SADCC	Southern African Development Co-ordination Conference
SIDS	Small Island Developing States
SPARTECA	South Pacific Regional Trade and Economic Co-operation Agreement
SPF	South Pacific Forum
TRIMs	Trade Related Investment Measures
TRIPs	Trade Related Intellectual Property Rights
UNCED	United Nations Conference on the Environment and Development
UNCTAD	United Nations Conference on Trade and Development
UNCLOS	United Nations Convention on the Law of the Sea
UNDRO	United Nations Disaster Relief Organisation
UR	Uruguay Round – General Agreement on Tariffs and Trade
WTO	World Trade Organisation

Index

*Locations in **bold** indicate tables.*